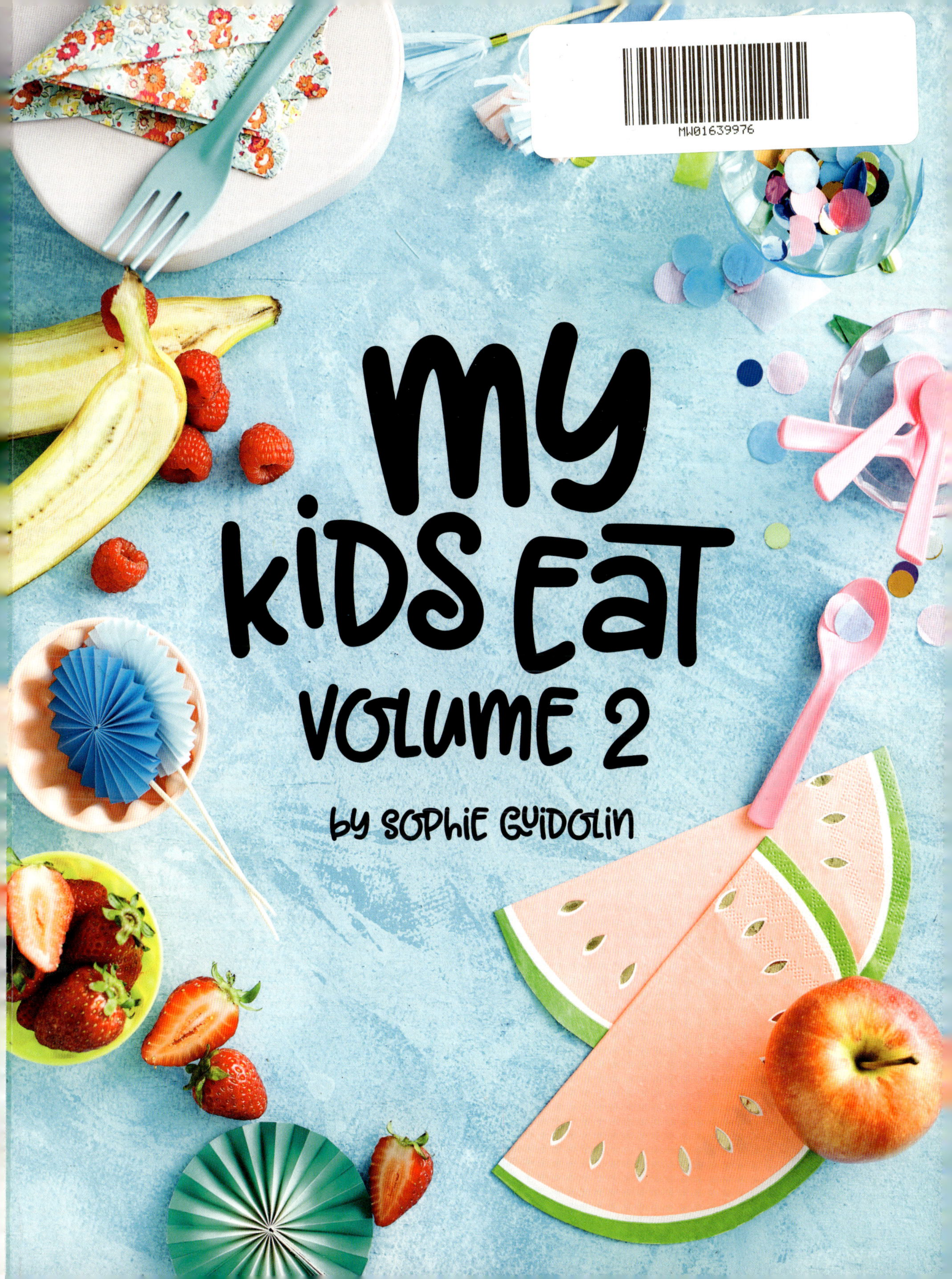
MW01639976
my
kiDS Eat
VOLUME 2
by SOPHIE GUIDOLIN

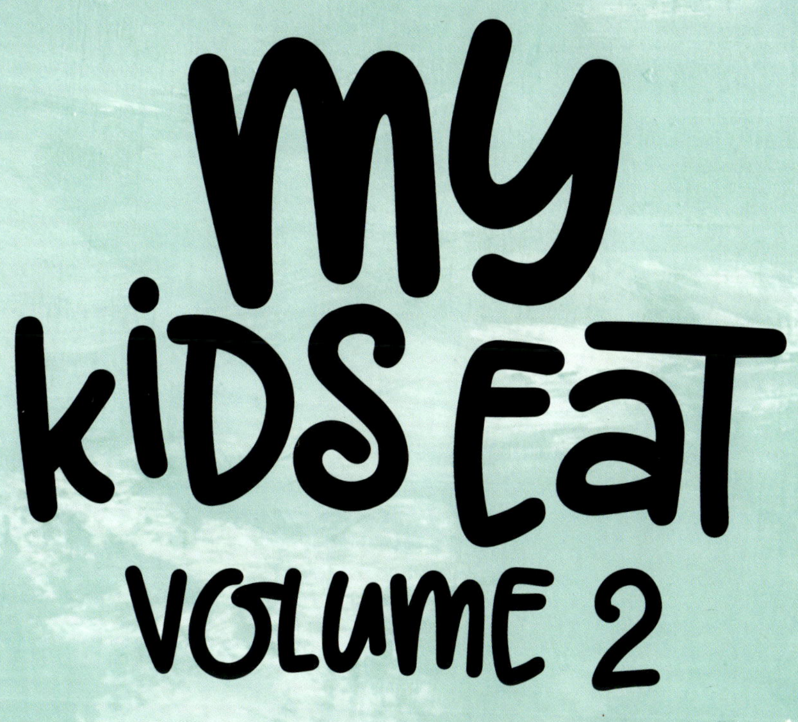

by Sophie Guidolin

NOURISH YOUR TRIBE WITH MORE THAN
65 KID-APPROVED WHOLEFOOD RECIPES

CONTENTS

WELCOME to MY KIDS EAT VOLUME 2

THE original *My Kids Eat* recipe book was developed over four years. After having my first two children (Kai and Ryder), I realised that allowing them to feel empowered with their food choices was an integral part of them actually eating healthier. My theory behind *My Kids Eat* was to create a recipe book aimed at kids, for kids. All of the recipes and food styling were themed with children in mind. I wanted them to flick through the pages and be excited about choosing their breakfast, lunch or dinner. The key, however, was to ensure that all the options were great, healthy ones.

After having our twins and growing from a family of four to six, I felt it was natural to update the original *My Kids Eat*, which was written when the boys were aged between two and three. I wanted to include recipes that families would love all the way through to those early teen years too.

Our boys are now a lot more hands-on in the kitchen, and some of these recipes are their own creations, which I am very excited about! I am always encouraging their love of cooking and furthering their nutritional knowledge, so they are able to make better choices for their own goals as pre-teens passionate about sport.

"WHEN EATING OUR MAIN MEALS, WE ALWAYS STRIVE TO EAT TOGETHER AS A FAMILY AND, IMPORTANTLY, WE ALL EAT THE SAME MEALS."

A lot of the recipes in this book are fairly straightforward and easy to make, which means the kids can help you with cooking. Introducing children to food and cooking at an early age will start them on the road to thinking about what they eat, which in turn will help them make more informed choices when it comes to food.

My kids are now three (our twin girls), nine and ten. With my older two, I am now allowing them the freedom to cook more of their own meals and make their own lunches. This not only encourages their love of cooking as well as their independence, but

also expands their food knowledge. They often make dinner once a week, and they make smarter choices when preparing their school lunches and choosing healthy snacks to eat with the girls. Some of their favourite meals to make include nachos, tacos, pizzas, lasagne, pasta and baked goodies!

Allowing children the freedom to cook can be overwhelming for parents – from wasted ingredients to the mess, it can all seem too hard. But like everything in life, we must practise in order to improve. By allowing your kids to mess up the kitchen, crack two dozen eggs for a recipe that only needs two, and have a few 'my cake didn't rise!' moments, it teaches them valuable cooking skills and allows them to discover new talents. After all, mess can be cleaned and the skills they will learn will last a lifetime!

When eating our main meals, we always strive to eat together as a family and, importantly, we all eat the same meals. This has had a big impact on our children's choices and diet. We find that with our youngest kids, they always want what we are having – no matter what it is (why is it that someone else's food always tastes better?). For this reason, you will find that a lot of the recipes here are designed as family meals rather than a single serving.

While we all eat the same meal, we do allow our children to have their own taste preferences. However, we encourage them to first try the meal before deciding if they want to add anything extra (lemon, salt, pepper, sauces etc.). This has really helped develop our children's tastes, and at present (touch wood!) there are very few things the kids won't eat. We also have the rule that if you don't like a meal, you don't have to eat it, but we also won't substitute it with anything else. This means we're not cooking different meals to suit everyone. It also means that our kids usually eat every meal served.

At present in Australia, 27% of children are overweight or obese, which is an alarming statistic. I believe that if we placed a greater emphasis on nutritional choices and an active lifestyle rather than physical attributes, we would see an incredible improvement in the health and wellbeing of our children. Educating children in school about nutrition should be a focus. This would be a more effective approach to tackling the issue of childhood obesity, by preventing it as opposed to treating it. As parents, we have the power to change the future through our children.

My hope is that this book will inspire more children to get involved and feel empowered in the kitchen, from toddlers making their first food choices right through to teens cooking a family dinner.

SOPHiE 

TIPS & TRICKS

HERE ARE SOME OF MY TRIED AND TESTED TIPS TO HELP DEVELOP YOUR CHILD'S PALATE, ENCOURAGE THEIR LOVE OF FOOD AND EXPAND THEIR NUTRITIONAL KNOWLEDGE, SO YOU CAN MAKE HEALTHIER CHOICES TOGETHER EVERY DAY.

MEALTIME 101

Make mealtimes a fun family social occasion. Sit down, engage with your kids and relax. We have a tradition in our house where we play Top Three, Bottom Three, which is the kids' top three highlights and low points of their day. By doing this I gain an insight into their day and anything that might be bothering them. Everyone has different taste buds; however, as parents, kids want to be exactly like us. I make a very big effort to not say I don't like something because, in most cases, if you say you don't like it they won't either – before they have even tried it. Think about the foods you don't really like now – did your parents not eat that food, or was there a defining moment that you recall not liking it?

FUSSY EATERS

When parents make dinner four times until their child will eat, not only is the parent cooking multiple meals but the power is given to the toddler. If my kids don't want the dinner that I've made, I don't make them eat it, but they must stay at the table, and I won't make them another meal. They will usually eat without any fuss. Kids like to push boundaries; sometimes the easiest option can set you up for a struggle later on.

SUPPLEMENTS

Often supplements for children can actually hinder your child's nutrition. When a supplement is, for example, a milk drink and it fills them up, parents might think that their child is getting their vitamins from that, so it's okay. However, nutrients are always best straight from the source – food! So while supplementation has its place, food should always be first choice.

HEALTHY HABITS

Family mealtimes can be tricky, with different schedules and bedtimes. But if you can, try to eat dinner together as a family regularly.

The 'eat everything on your plate' rule is a big no-no. It sets kids up to overeat rather than stopping when they're genuinely full. The sense of feeling full is an important sensation to feel and master as an adult.

Whenever I talk about nutrition with my kids, I only mention the health and energy benefits, and never fat or weight gain or loss. We need to educate our children about the importance of good nutrition, but the focus needs to be on the positives rather than the negatives.

When eating out, skip the kids' menu. Rarely does it include a nutritionally sound choice. Select from the normal menu and ask for a kids/entrée size.

Kitchen tasks

I ALWAYS FIND THAT KIDS WANT TO DO ANYTHING YOU'RE DOING, EAT WHAT YOU'RE EATING AND BE WITH YOU AT EVERY MOMENT. SO WHY NOT GET THEM INVOLVED? IT WILL ENCOURAGE THEIR INTEREST IN THE KITCHEN AND ALLOW YOU SOME TIME TO GRAB THE INGREDIENTS FOR THE NEXT STEP, WASH A BOWL OR MAKE A CUPPA!

AGES 2–3

This age group is more about getting started in the kitchen – finding utensils and sitting with you while you cook. Try:

- Selecting the right utensils
- Kneading dough
- Stirring
- Using cookie cutters
- Pouring in ingredients

AGES 3–5

This is an incredibly independent age where children often feel they can do a lot more than they are safely capable of doing. With supervision to ensure safety, tasks they can help with are:

- Whisking eggs
- Rinsing vegetables and fruits
- Mashing potatoes
- Measuring liquids and spoons
- Pulling herbs off stems

AGES 6–8

By this age kids understand the concept of sharp objects and danger, and they can read recipes and work out basic measurements. They will still need supervision. Try:

- Peeling and grating
- Cutting vegetables and fruits
- Using a can opener
- Boiling eggs
- Using the toaster
- Clearing the table
- Reading recipes and measuring ingredients

AGES 8–12

If your pre-teen is like mine, they think they can do anything! While they may feel invincible, they need direction to ensure they learn in a safe way, especially when using the oven and stovetop. Try:

- Operating the oven
- Baking cookies and bread
- Steaming rice
- Boiling pasta
- Using the food processor
- Using a knife to cut vegetables
- Cooking small, familiar meals
- Stacking/emptying dishwasher

AGES 13–18

This age group is about empowering your teenager to be self-reliant in the kitchen. Allowing your teen to cook will enable them to eat well as an adult. By now they should be able to help in these ways:

- Using kitchen appliances
- Cleaning
- Selecting recipes
- Going to the grocery store with you
- Making family dinners
- Adapting recipes to suit tastes and the servings required
- Learning what is in foods

A
APPLE
BROCCOLI
CARROT
HONEYDEW
MELON
THE
A-Z
OF FRUIT & VEGGIES
I
ICEBERG
LETTUCE
HOW MANY FRUITS AND VEGGIES CAN YOU THINK OF FOR EACH LETTER OF THE ALPHABET? HERE ARE A FEW FROM AROUND THE WORLD TO GET YOU STARTED!
nectarine
onion
ugli fruit
VANILLA
BEAN
SNOW
PEAS
tomato
V

Dates
fig
GARLIC
E
EGGPLANT
LEMONS
& LIMES
MUSHROOM
jalapeño
kiwifruit
P
PUMPKIN
Quince
RADISH
WATERMELON
X
XIMENIA
yam
ZUCCHINI

Fast healthy brekkies

RICOTTA PANCAKES WITH STRAWBERRIES

PREP + COOK TIME 20 MINUTES SERVES 4–6

⅔ cup (160g) ricotta
½ cup (125ml) milk
4 eggs, separated
⅓ cup (80ml) honey or pure maple syrup
1 teaspoon vanilla extract
1⅓ cups (200g) wholemeal self-raising flour
½ cup (90g) finely chopped strawberries (see Swap It)
cooking-oil spray
¾ cup (180g) ricotta, extra
160g strawberries, extra, halved (see Swap It)
2 tablespoons coarsely chopped almonds
1 tablespoon honey or pure maple syrup, extra

1 Whisk ricotta, milk, egg yolks, honey and vanilla in a small bowl. Stir in flour and chopped strawberries.

2 Beat egg whites in a small bowl with an electric mixer until soft peaks form. Fold through ricotta mixture in two batches.

3 Spray a medium frying pan with oil; heat over medium heat. Spoon ¼ cupfuls of batter into pan (see Tip); cook pancakes for 3 minutes each side or until golden. Repeat with remaining mixture to make 10 pancakes in total.

4 Serve pancakes with extra ricotta, extra strawberries and almonds; drizzle with extra honey.

You may need to slightly spread the pancake batter with the back of a spoon if it doesn't spread when you add it to the frying pan. These pancakes are also great for dessert.

SWAP IT!
Swap the strawberries for bananas or blueberries, if you like.

FOOD FACT!
Tomatoes are a rich source of vitamin C, an antioxidant that prevents the nasty toxins from damaging your body's systems.

HUMPTY DUMPTY TOAST WITH TOMATO

PREP + COOK TIME 10 MINUTES **SERVES** 4

- 4 thick slices wholegrain bread (280g) (see Tip)
- 40g butter
- 250g mixed cherry truss and grape tomatoes
- 4 eggs

This recipe is good for using up slightly stale bread or bread rolls. Split rolls in half before cooking.

1 Cut 6cm rounds from centre of the bread slices, using either a cutter or an upturned glass. Heat half the butter in a medium frying pan; cook 2 bread slices and round cut-outs for 1 minute or until browned lightly underneath.
2 Meanwhile, add half the tomatoes to edge of pan and cook until softened slightly.
3 Turn bread. Crack 2 eggs into holes in bread; cook over low-medium heat for 3 minutes or until egg whites are set and yolks are cooked to your liking. Bread slices can be turned again to set the tops, if you like. Keep warm.
4 Repeat with remaining butter, bread, tomatoes and eggs.
5 Serve toast with bread cut-outs and tomatoes, seasoned with freshly ground pepper.

MAN ON THE MOON OMELETTES

PREP + COOK TIME 10 MINUTES SERVES 4

8 eggs
⅓ cup (80ml) water
20g coconut oil

1 Prepare chosen filling ingredients; see right for ideas.
2 Beat eggs and the water in a large bowl with a balloon whisk or fork until combined. Season.
3 Heat a quarter of the oil in a small frying pan over medium heat. When oil is hot, add a quarter of the egg mixture. Using a wide spatula, gently push the set egg mixture toward the centre of pan; tilt the pan, allowing the uncooked egg mixture to run onto the base of the pan. Repeat pushing and tilting about three times until egg is just set.
4 Place a quarter of the filling over one half of the omelette. Fold one side of the omelette over using the spatula. Slide onto a plate. Repeat to make a total of four omelettes, wiping out the pan with paper towel before making each one.

SHROOMS & CHEESE
Heat 30g butter in a large frying pan over high heat; cook 250g sliced button mushrooms, stirring, for 5 minutes or until browned. Season. Divide mushrooms, 80g crumbled feta and ¼ cup basil among omelettes.

CHICKEN & SPINACH
Thinly slice 250g cooked chicken breast. Divide chicken and 60g baby spinach leaves among omelettes.

FOOD FACT!
Omega-3 essential fatty acids are critical in a child's brain function and development. The best sources? Eggs, nuts, high-quality meats and fish.

DID YOU KNOW?
Cacao powder is raw cold-pressed cocoa beans. It is not the same as cocoa powder, which is roasted at a high temperature, lowering the overall nutritional value.

BANANA BLAST WITH CACAO CRUNCH

PREP + COOK TIME 10 MINUTES (+ COOLING) **SERVES** 4

2 cups (500ml) milk (see Tip)
2 medium bananas (400g), chopped coarsely (see Tip)
½ cup (140g) Greek-style yoghurt (see Tip)
1 tablespoon honey or pure maple syrup
1 tablespoon white chia seeds
½ teaspoon ground cinnamon

CACAO CRUNCH

¼ cup (90g) honey
2 teaspoons coconut oil
1 tablespoon cacao powder
2 cups (45g) puffed corn, rice or millet
¼ cup (40g) chopped almonds

1 Make cacao crunch.

2 Blend or process all ingredients until smooth.

3 Divide smoothie among glasses. Serve sprinkled with cacao crunch.

cacao crunch Heat honey and oil in a medium pan until foamy. Stir in cacao, puffs and almonds. Spread onto a tray; cool. Store in an airtight container for up to 3 days. Makes 3 cups.

For a dairy-free option, use soy, rice, coconut or nut milk and soy or coconut yoghurt. Use frozen bananas or add ice cubes to the blender for a thicker smoothie. Drizzle a teaspoon of honey on the inside of glasses before filling, if you like.

FOOD FACT!
Acai berries contain more antioxidants than blueberries, strawberries and cranberries!
1/3 CUP

Acai Berry Bowl

PREP TIME 10 MINUTES (+ FREEZING) **SERVES** 4

- 2 medium bananas (400g), chopped coarsely (see Tip)
- ½ cup (75g) frozen blueberries
- 100g frozen unsweetened pure acai puree (see Tip)
- 1 cup (280g) Greek-style or coconut yoghurt
- 2 teaspoons honey
- ⅓ cup (50g) fresh raspberries
- 2 tablespoons fresh blueberries
- 2 tablespoons mixed seeds or chopped nuts

1 Place banana in an airtight container or resealable plastic bag. Freeze for 4 hours until firm.

2 Blend frozen banana with frozen blueberries, acai, yoghurt and honey until smooth.

3 Pour into serving bowls. Top with fresh berries and seeds. Serve immediately.

SERVING SUGGESTION

You might like to top the bowl with the cacao crunch on page 21.

TIP *Freeze the bananas overnight. Acai puree can be found in the freezer section of some supermarkets and health food stores.*

BERRY BIRCHER

PREP TIME 20 MINUTES (+ REFRIGERATION) **SERVES** 4

1⅓ cups (120g) rolled oats
pinch ground cinnamon
1 tablespoon white chia seeds
¾ cup (180ml) unsweetened apple juice
¾ cup (200g) Greek-style or coconut yoghurt (see Swap It)
1 medium apple (150g) (see Swap It)
125g fresh berries
1 medium apple (150g), extra, sliced (see Swap It)
2 tablespoons natural flaked almonds (optional)
2 tablespoons pepitas (pumpkin seed kernels)
1 tablespoon pure maple syrup (optional) (see Swap It)

1 Combine oats, cinnamon, chia, juice and yoghurt in a medium bowl. Cover; refrigerate for 15 minutes until thickened, or overnight.

2 Coarsely grate apple and stir through muesli. Divide among four bowls; top with berries, extra apple, almonds and pepitas. Serve with maple syrup. The mixture will thicken on standing; add a spoonful of extra yoghurt or a little milk, if needed.

Make a double batch to save time; the muesli will keep at the end of step 1 for up to 3 days in the fridge.

SWAP IT!
You could also use coconut cream or coconut water instead of the yoghurt. Try a pear or carrot in place of the apple and top with fruit in season. Swap honey for the maple syrup.

FOOD FACT!
An avocado is 75% water, and just a quarter of one contains 2g fibre, as well as 30% of your daily folate and 25% of your daily vitamin C requirements.

SUPERSEED AVO SMASH

PREP + COOK TIME 5 MINUTES SERVES 2

- 1 tablespoon pepitas (pumpkin seed kernels)
- 1 tablespoon sunflower seeds
- 1 teaspoon sesame seeds
- 4 slices wholegrain sourdough bread (120g), toasted
- ½ large avocado (160g)
- 250g mini roma, grape or cherry tomatoes, halved
- 1 tablespoon finely chopped fresh basil

1 Place seeds in a dry small frying pan; stir seeds over medium heat for 2 minutes or until they are browned lightly and fragrant. Remove from pan.

2 Meanwhile, toast bread. Spread avocado over toast and top with tomato; season with salt. Sprinkle with seeds and chopped basil.

SERVING SUGGESTION

Crumble 30g feta or goat's cheese per serve over toast for a protein boost.

If you prefer the tomatoes warm, heat 1 teaspoon olive oil in the same pan after seeds are removed. Add tomato and cook for 1–2 minutes, shaking the pan occasionally, until they are softened.

THIS IS A FAVOURITE FOR MY KIDS AND I LOVE THAT IT PACKS A FLAVOUR AND NUTRIENT PUNCH. AND IT'S EASY ENOUGH FOR KIDS TO MAKE!

Monster muesli trifles

PREP TIME 20 MINUTES SERVES 4

1 medium mango (430g) (see Swap It)
250g strawberries, quartered (see Swap It)
2 cups (560g) Greek-style or coconut yoghurt

MONSTER MUESLI

2 cups (180g) rolled oats
½ cup (80g) sultanas
¼ cup (35g) dried cranberries
¼ cup (50g) pepitas (pumpkin seed kernels)
½ cup (40g) shredded coconut
1 tablespoon ground cinnamon
1 teaspoon ground nutmeg
¼ cup (45g) black chia seeds

1 Make monster muesli.

2 Cut cheeks from mango; scoop the flesh from cheeks and chop coarsely. Combine mango and strawberries in a small bowl.

3 Divide fruit among four 1½-cup (375ml) glasses. Top with yoghurt, then ¼ cup monster muesli on each serve.

monster muesli Place all ingredients in a medium airtight container; mix together with your hands. This amount of muesli serves 8; you only need 1 cup for this recipe. Seal the remainder in the container and store at room temperature for up to 1 month.

SWAP IT!
You can substitute your favourite fruit for the mangoes and strawberries.

FOOD FACT!

An egg a day will assist your child in meeting all their nutrient needs, with protein, lutein, choline, omega-3s and more!

Eggy Toast

PREP + COOK TIME 12 MINUTES MAKES 8 SLICES

4 eggs
1 cup (250ml) milk
40g butter or coconut oil
8 slices day-old sourdough or wholegrain bread (360g) (see Tip)
pure maple syrup and berries, or tomato sauce, to serve

1 Lightly beat eggs and milk in a medium bowl to combine.
2 Melt 2 teaspoons of the butter in a medium frying pan over medium-high heat.
3 Dip bread slices, one at a time, into egg mixture. Cook in batches of two at a time (or as many as will fit in the pan). Cook for 1 minute each side or until golden. Transfer to a plate; cover to keep warm. Wipe pan clean with paper towel. Repeat with remaining butter, egg mixture and bread to make eight slices in total.
4 Serve with maple syrup and berries, or with tomato sauce.

Use any type of bread for this recipe.

CHEESY FRENCH TOAST

Add ½ cup grated parmesan or cheddar and 2 tablespoons chopped fresh chives or parsley to the egg mixture in step 1.

VEGAN FRENCH TOAST

Skip step 1 and instead mash 1 very ripe banana in a bowl with a fork. Gradually stir in a 400ml can coconut milk. Continue from step 2, using coconut oil to fry. Serve with fruit or maple syrup.

Lunch box ideas

Lunch on the Run

When packing lunchboxes, there are a few key things I always I do:

- Have a frozen ice pack in there to keep foods at a tasty – and safe – temperature
- Use an insulated lunchbox or bag
- Freeze baked goods in individual portions; they will defrost by recess, making it easy to grab-and-go.

Another tip is to pack lunch first, before packing snacks – I always want my kids to have the three major macronutrient groups in their lunch: protein, carbohydrates and fats.

Remember that pre-teens need more food than younger children. My boys often have varying appetites in accordance with their growth cycles. Some days they're starving and will eat three servings; on other days they barely touch their food. This is normal, depending on their activity or even what food they ate that day. I try to load them up on carbs as they're very athletic and will go until they crash. I always include a protein, which assists with recovery, and healthy fats, such as avocado and eggs.

Try to avoid empty calories, or foods that have little nutritional value, such as potato chips, lollies, and ice-blocks from the canteen. Instead, fill them up with foods that are HIGH in nutritional value, with necessary minerals and vitamins.

My kids are loving wraps right now. They're easy, I can pack them with vegetables and they don't get soggy throughout the day. I use chicken breast that I have already cooked and stored in the fridge, which cuts down on preparation time.

NIBBLES
Our school stops for a brain-food snack, mid-morning. For this I pack carrot sticks, sultanas, dried fruit, banana, apple etc.
The other winner is frittata. A great filling combo is pumpkin, spinach, tomato and chicken. When I pack frittatas, I usually include some crackers or an additional carbohydrate source too.
With lunch sorted, move onto morning tea. Usually kids don't get a whole lot of time to eat morning tea, so I like to make this a fast, delicious part of the lunchbox – most times this is banana bread for us. It's full of carbs, tastes delicious and is easy and quick to eat. Homemade pikelets are also an epic choice and usually a winner.
We are loving savoury muffins. We use the same base recipe but vary it depending upon what leftovers are in the fridge. Bolognese sauce? Tick! Tuna mornay? Tick! Roast veggies? Tick! They're all perfect for the lunchbox.
WATER
Water, always. I pack large bottles for the boys and have water on-hand for the twins also.

Banana & Walnut Bread

PREP + COOK TIME 1 HOUR MAKES 10 SLICES

- ½ cup (60g) coconut flour
- ½ teaspoon bicarbonate of soda
- ½ teaspoon Himalayan salt
- ⅓ cup (35g) chopped walnuts (see Tip)
- 1 large overripe banana (230g)
- ¼ cup (35g) chopped pitted dried dates
- 6 eggs
- ¼ cup (50g) coconut oil
- 1 teaspoon vanilla extract
- ¼ cup (70g) Greek-style yoghurt (see Tip)
- ¼ cup (60ml) almond, oat or rice milk (see Tip)

1 Preheat oven to 180°C. Grease a 10.5cm x 24.5cm loaf pan (inside top measurement); line base and long sides with two layers of baking paper.

2 Combine the flour, soda, salt and walnuts in a large bowl.

3 Process the banana and dates until smooth. Add the eggs to the processor with oil, vanilla, yoghurt and milk. Process until just combined, being careful not to overwork the mixture.

4 Add the banana mixture to the dry ingredients; stir until combined. Pour mixture into the pan.

5 Bake loaf for 45 minutes or until a skewer inserted in the centre, but not through a crack, comes out clean. Turn, top-side up, onto a wire rack to cool.

For a nut-free option for school, replace the walnuts with cacao nibs and use oat or rice milk. This bread is gluten-free; use a coconut or soy yoghurt to make it dairy-free too. Cut loaf into slices, wrap them individually and freeze, ready to pop into lunchboxes.

FOOD FACT!

Bananas have higher levels of antioxidants as they ripen. The riper the banana, the higher the glycaemic index and the sweeter the bread will be.

FOOD FACT!
Quinoa is gluten-free, high in protein, includes almost twice as much fibre as other grains and contains all nine essential amino acids.

CHOCOLATE QUINOA MUFFINS

PREP + COOK TIME **30 MINUTES (+ COOLING)** **MAKES** **12**

2 cups (250g) quinoa flour (see Tip)
2 teaspoons gluten-free baking powder
⅓ cup (35g) organic raw cacao powder
½ cup (175g) honey
½ cup (100g) coconut oil, melted
⅔ cup (160ml) soy or almond milk (see Tip)
1 teaspoon vanilla extract
2 eggs, beaten lightly

1 Preheat oven to 160°C. Line a 12-hole (⅓-cup/80ml) muffin pan with paper cases, or use a silicone muffin pan.
2 Sift the flour, baking powder and cacao into a large bowl. Add the honey, oil, milk, vanilla and eggs. Using a large metal spoon, stir until just combined – don't overmix. Spoon mixture into paper cases.
3 Bake muffins for 20 minutes or until a skewer inserted in the centre of one comes out clean. Stand in the pan for 5 minutes before transferring to a wire rack to cool. Wrap cooled muffins individually and freeze, ready to pop into lunchboxes.

For lighter muffins, use 1 cup (125g) quinoa flour and 1 cup (150g) self-raising flour; however, these will not be gluten-free. These muffins are dairy-free. For a nut-free option, or if making for school, use soy milk.

CHEWY MUESLI BARS

PREP + COOK TIME 40 MINUTES (+ STANDING) **MAKES** 16

- 2 cups (180g) rolled oats
- ¾ cup (60g) desiccated coconut
- ½ cup (80g) wholemeal plain flour
- ¼ cup (50g) pepitas (pumpkin seed kernels) (see Swap It)
- ¼ cup (35g) sunflower seeds
- ¼ cup (40g) sultanas
- ¼ cup (30g) chopped dried apricots
- 1 teaspoon bicarbonate of soda
- ¼ teaspoon sea salt flakes
- ½ cup (100g) coconut oil
- ½ cup (125ml) rice malt syrup
- ½ teaspoon vanilla extract

1 Preheat oven to 170°C. Grease a 20cm x 30cm slice pan; line base with baking paper, extending paper 5cm over long sides of pan.

2 Combine dry ingredients in a large bowl.

3 Place oil and syrup in a small saucepan; bring to the boil. Boil until oil is melted. Remove from heat; stir in vanilla.

4 Add oil mixture to dry mixture; stir thoroughly to combine (the mixture will be quite firm; use clean hands to combine, if necessary). Spoon mixture into pan and press down firmly with a spatula or damp hands to level.

5 Bake for 25 minutes or until golden. Turn off oven; leave slice in oven for a further 5 minutes to dry out slightly. Remove from oven; stand slice in pan for 15 minutes.

6 Use the baking paper to help lift the slice onto a wire rack. Cool completely. Remove paper; cut slice into 16 fingers.

Bars will keep in an airtight container for up to 1 week. If they become sticky, place in a 150°C oven for 5 minutes; turn the oven off and leave for a further 5 minutes.

SWAP IT!

Nuts are a great source of healthy fats but many schools are nut-free. Swap some of the fruit or seeds for nuts if enjoying these at home.

SWAP IT!
Fritters can be made with grated carrot or a mixture of zucchini, corn and carrot. Use gluten-free plain flour, if you prefer.

I OFTEN SERVE THESE FRITTERS FOR BREAKFAST, MORNING TEA OR IN LUNCHBOXES. THEY'RE HAND-HELD AND EASY TO EAT ON THE GO!

ZUCCHINI FRITTERS

PREP + COOK TIME 15 MINUTES MAKES 10

- 2 large zucchini (300g) (see Swap It)
- 3 eggs, beaten lightly
- 2 tablespoons chopped chives
- ¼ teaspoon Himalayan salt
- 2 tablespoons wholemeal plain flour (see Swap It)
- 2 tablespoons coconut oil

Fritters make a great lunchbox or after-school snack. They will keep for up to 3 days, covered, in the fridge.

1 Grate the zucchini coarsely. Squeeze excess liquid from the zucchini, in small amounts, using your hands. Combine zucchini with remaining ingredients, except the oil, in a medium bowl.

2 Heat half the oil in a large frying pan over medium heat. Drop 2 tablespoons of mixture into pan; spread slightly into rounds. Cook fritters for 2 minutes each side or until browned and cooked through. Drain on paper towel. Repeat with remaining oil and zucchini mixture to make 10 fritters in total.

SERVING SUGGESTIONS

Serve fritters with lettuce and tomato relish, or put them in a wrap with hummus and spinach or tabbouleh for a more substantial lunch. For a delicious breakfast, top with poached eggs.

The Chicken & The Egg

PREP + COOK TIME 25 MINUTES MAKES 12

150g cooked chicken, chopped coarsely (see Swap It)
100g feta cheese
¼ cup (20g) finely grated parmesan cheese
⅓ cup chopped fresh basil
7 eggs
½ cup (125ml) milk
18 grape tomatoes (135g)
grape tomatoes and fresh basil leaves, extra, to serve (optional)

1 Preheat oven to 180°C. Line a 12-hole (⅓-cup/80ml) muffin pan with paper muffin cases, or cut squares of baking paper and press them into the pan holes.
2 Divide chicken, crumbled feta, parmesan and chopped basil evenly among pan holes.
3 Whisk eggs and milk in a large jug until well combined; season. Pour the egg mixture into pan holes.
4 Cut tomatoes in half lengthways. Place three tomato halves on top of each frittata. Bake for 20 minutes or until just set.
5 Serve frittatas with extra tomatoes and basil leaves.

These are perfect for lunchboxes or an easy breakfast on the go. Fussy eater? Puree the tomato, chicken and basil for a smooth texture!

SWAP IT!
You can swap the chicken for tuna, salmon or leftover roast vegetables from dinner.

SWAP IT!
If eating at home, you can use peanut butter instead of the nut-free butter. Always choose a nut-free butter for the lunchbox.

REMEMBER THAT WE OFTEN EAT WITH ALL OF OUR SENSES; ENCOURAGE FUSSY EATERS WITH COLOUR, FLAVOUR AND FUN!

Pikelet faces

PREP + COOK TIME 30 MINUTES MAKES 15

1 cup (150g) wholemeal spelt flour
2 teaspoons baking powder
pinch bicarbonate of soda
2 tablespoons honey or pure maple syrup
1 egg, beaten lightly
¾ cup (180ml) milk, approximately
nut-free butter (see Swap It), cream cheese and fresh fruit, to decorate (optional)

1 Sift dry ingredients into a medium bowl; return husks to bowl. Make a well in the centre; gradually stir in honey, egg and enough milk to make a smooth, creamy, pouring consistency.

2 Drop dessertspoons of batter from the tip of the spoon into a heated greased frying pan, allowing room for spreading. When bubbles begin to appear, turn pikelets over (see Tip); cook until golden on the other side.

3 Decorate pikelets with butter, cream cheese and fresh fruit to resemble faces.

You can pour the batter into a squeezy sauce bottle and write the kids' names or a message with the batter. Turn pikelets just before the bubbles burst for best results. Pikelets will keep for 2 days and can be frozen for up to 2 months.

I LOVE A PICK-AND-MIX SALAD – THE KIDS CAN EAT THE RAINBOW!

SHAKE-IT MEXICHICKEN

PREP + COOK TIME 20 MINUTES **SERVES** 4

- 500g chicken breast fillets
- 2 teaspoons sweet paprika
- 1 teaspoon ground cumin
- 1 teaspoon dried oregano
- 1 teaspoon garlic powder
- 1 tablespoon olive oil
- 2 medium corn cobs (800g), husks and silks removed
- 1 large avocado (320g), mashed
- ¼ cup (60ml) lime or lemon juice
- ⅓ cup (100g) Greek-style yoghurt
- 400g can black beans or red kidney beans, drained, rinsed
- ½ small red onion (50g), sliced thinly
- 250g mixed cherry tomatoes, halved
- 2 baby cos lettuce, leaves torn

1 Combine chicken, spices and oil in a large bowl; toss to coat. Cook chicken and corn on a heated oiled grill plate (or barbecue or grill) over medium-high heat for 5 minutes each side or until cooked through. Slice chicken thickly. Cut kernels from cobs.

2 Blend avocado, juice and yoghurt with a hand-held blender in a jug; season to taste with salt. Divide avocado mixture between four serving containers.

3 Layer beans, chicken, corn, onion, tomato and lettuce over avocado mixture in containers (use non-breakable containers for children); seal. Refrigerate or keep cold with a freezer brick.

4 Shake or toss salad just before serving.

SERVING SUGGESTION

For adults, try adding some sprigs of coriander and some sliced fresh chilli or dried chilli flakes.

FOOD FACT!
Red kidney beans have a high content of complex carbohydrates and dietary fibre, which helps to lower cholesterol levels in the blood.
salad

FOOD FACT!
Chickpeas are high in various nutrients, particularly fibre, which supports a healthy digestive system.

Green Hummus & Bread Chips

PREP + COOK TIME 12 MINUTES **MAKES** 3 CUPS

1 cup (120g) frozen peas
2 x 400g cans chickpeas
1 clove garlic, crushed
¼ cup (70g) tahini
¼ cup (60ml) lemon juice
¼ cup (60ml) olive oil
vegetable sticks, to serve

BREAD CHIPS
4 pieces Mountain Bread (100g)
olive oil cooking spray

1 Make bread chips.
2 Meanwhile, place peas in a heatproof bowl; cover with boiling water. Stand for 3 minutes; drain. Drain chickpeas over a bowl; reserve ½ cup of the liquid.
3 Process chickpeas, peas, garlic, tahini, juice and oil until smooth. Add reserved liquid gradually, if needed. Season to taste with salt.
4 Serve hummus with bread chips and vegetable sticks.
bread chips Preheat oven to 180°C. Place bread on oven trays. Spray lightly with oil. Bake for 5 minutes or until crisp. Cool, break into pieces.

SERVING SUGGESTION

The hummus can also be served as a dip with meatballs or used in wraps or sandwiches.

Hummus will keep for up to 1 week in the fridge. Bread chips will keep in an airtight container for 1 week.

CHOCOCONUT COOKIES

PREP + COOK TIME 30 MINUTES MAKES 16

- 2 cups (160g) desiccated coconut
- 1 cup (130g) wholemeal spelt flour
- 2 tablespoons white chia seeds
- 1 teaspoon ground cinnamon
- 6 fresh dates (120g), pitted, halved
- ¼ cup (50g) coconut oil, melted
- ½ cup (170g) rice malt syrup
- 1 egg yolk
- 2 teaspoons vanilla extract
- ½ cup (50g) cacao nibs (see Tip) or chopped dark chocolate (70% cocoa)

1 Preheat oven to 160°C. Line two large oven trays with baking paper.

2 Process coconut, flour, seeds, cinnamon, dates, oil, syrup, egg yolk and vanilla until well combined. Transfer to a medium bowl; stir in cacao nibs.

3 Roll 2 tablespoons of mixture into balls and place on tray; flatten with the palm of your hand into 8cm rounds.

4 Bake for 12 minutes or until golden brown. Cool on trays.

Cacao nibs are both textural and chocolaty with no sweetness. They can be found at some supermarkets and health food stores. Cookies will keep in a sealed jar for up to 1 week or freeze for up to 2 months. These cookies are nut-free and dairy-free.

COOKIES
Sweets

DID YOU KNOW?
Pumpkins can be yellow, green, white, even blue!

Roast beef pumpkin rolls

PREP + COOK TIME 30 MINUTES SERVES 2

200g pumpkin, chopped coarsely (see Tip)
olive oil cooking spray
1½ teaspoons dukkah (optional)
2 wholemeal rye or wholemeal bread rolls (100g) (see Tip)
2 tablespoons hummus
125g roast beef or cooked chicken, sliced
20g baby spinach or rocket leaves

1 Preheat oven to 220°C. Line an oven tray with baking paper.
2 Place pumpkin on tray. Spray with oil and sprinkle with dukkah. Bake for 25 minutes or until tender; mash roughly with a fork.
3 Cut rolls in half. Spread hummus over cut sides of rolls. Divide pumpkin between roll bases. Top with beef, spinach and roll tops.

SERVING SUGGESTION
For adults, try adding a scatter of chilli flakes and some sliced red onion.

You can also use roasted sweet potato instead of the pumpkin. The next time you roast beef, chicken or pumpkin, make extra for lunch the next day. For a gluten-free option, use gluten-free wraps or bread rolls.

Chicken 'Sushi' Rolls

PREP + COOK TIME 15 MINUTES SERVES 4

4 chicken tenderloins (300g)
1 tablespoon soy sauce
1 tablespoon honey
2 teaspoons coconut oil
8 large slices square wholemeal bread (360g)
¼ cup (75g) mayonnaise
2 sheets nori, quartered
4 baby cucumbers (160g)
½ medium avocado (125g)

Cook the chicken and prepare the remaining ingredients, except avocado, the night before. Assemble rolls close to serving.

1 Toss chicken in combined soy sauce and honey in a small bowl. Heat oil in a small frying pan over medium heat. Add chicken; cook for 2 minutes each side or until just cooked through. Remove from pan. Cool. Cut tenderloins in half lengthways.

2 Trim crusts from bread. Roll bread with a rolling pin to flatten. Spread bread with mayonnaise and top with nori. Cut cucumbers in quarters lengthways; cut avocado into eight slices lengthways.

3 Divide chicken, cucumber and avocado among bread slices; roll up to enclose. Cut each roll into four pieces.

SERVING SUGGESTION

For adults, try spreading the bread with a little wasabi paste; add some shredded green onion and sprinkle with some toasted sesame seeds.

FOOD FACT!

Nori sheets are high in B12, which benefits the central nervous system, and iodine, which is crucial for normal growth and development of the body.

Yummy Cheesy Pasta Slice

PREP + COOK TIME 50 MINUTES MAKES 16 PIECES

- 1 cup (220g) risoni pasta
- 500g broccoli, trimmed, cut into small florets (see Swap It)
- 1 cup (160g) frozen corn kernels, thawed (see Swap It)
- 250g haloumi, grated coarsely
- 4 green onions (100g), chopped finely
- 1 clove garlic, crushed
- ⅓ cup (25g) finely grated parmesan
- 4 eggs, beaten lightly
- ½ cup (75g) self-raising flour

1 Cook risoni in a medium saucepan of boiling salted water for 7 minutes or until almost tender. Add broccoli; boil for a further 1 minute. Drain pasta and broccoli; cool.

2 Preheat oven to 180°C. Grease a 20cm x 30cm slice pan; line base and long sides with baking paper, extending the paper 5cm over sides.

3 Place pasta and broccoli in a large bowl. Add corn, half the haloumi, onion, garlic, parmesan and egg; stir to combine. Add flour; stir well to combine. Season with salt and pepper.

4 Pour mixture into prepared pan; smooth top. Sprinkle with remaining haloumi. Bake for 40 minutes or until firm and cooked through. Cool in pan for 15 minutes before cutting into 16 pieces.

SERVING SUGGESTION

For adults, serve slice with chilli sauce and a mixed leaf salad for a more substantial meal.

Slice will keep in an airtight container in the fridge for up to 3 days.

SWAP IT!

Swap the vegetables to suit – try grated zucchini squeezed of excess liquid, chopped asparagus, grated carrot or peas.

Mix 'n' Match Muffins

PREP + COOK TIME 35 MINUTES **MAKES** 10

1½ cups (240g) wholemeal self-raising flour
½ cup (125ml) oat or almond milk
¼ cup (50g) coconut oil, melted
2 eggs, beaten lightly
choice of flavour add-in (see right; see Tip)

Muffins are best made on the day of serving. Keep muffins that contain meat or fish refrigerated or frozen.

1 Preheat oven to 180°C. Line 10 holes of a 12-hole (⅓-cup/80ml) muffin pan with paper cases or grease pan holes with coconut oil.
2 Mix all ingredients with your chosen flavour add-in in a medium bowl until just combined. Spoon mixture into cases.
3 Bake muffins for 25 minutes or until a skewer inserted into the centre of one comes out clean.

CHEESY VEGGIE FLAVOUR ADD-IN

Add 1 cup of grated carrot or zucchini, ½ cup mashed pumpkin and ½ cup grated cheddar cheese.
Optional: ½ cup corn kernels.

BOLOGNESE FLAVOUR ADD-IN

Add 1½ cups cooled bolognese sauce.
Optional: ½ cup grated cheddar or parmesan cheese.

TUNA MORNAY FLAVOUR ADD-IN

Add 1½ cups cooled tuna mornay.

Pizza Pinwheels

PREP + COOK TIME 35 MINUTES MAKES 12

1 cup (150g) self-raising flour
1 cup (160g) wholemeal self-raising flour
1 teaspoon salt
40g cold butter, chopped coarsely
¾ cup (180ml) buttermilk, approximately
1 cup (250ml) sauce or puree of your choice (see Tip)
½ small red onion (50g), chopped
½ small green capsicum (75g), chopped
100g mushrooms, sliced thinly (optional)
1 cup (120g) pizza cheese

1 Preheat oven to 220°C. Oil a 12-hole (⅓-cup/80ml) muffin pan.
2 Combine flours and salt in a medium bowl; rub in butter. Add enough buttermilk to mix to a soft, sticky dough. Turn dough onto a floured surface; knead lightly until smooth. Roll dough into a 30cm x 40cm rectangle.
3 Spread dough with sauce, leaving a 2cm border. Sprinkle with onion, capsicum, mushroom and half the cheese. Roll dough tightly from long side. Trim ends. Cut roll into 12 slices. Place scrolls, cut-side up, in pan. Sprinkle with remaining cheese.
4 Bake scrolls for 15 minutes or until cooked through. Eat warm or cooled.

CHICKEN & PESTO

In step 3, leave out the sauce and instead spread the dough with ½ cup pesto; top with 1 cup shredded cooked chicken. Add vegetables and cheese as above.

MEXICAN BEAN

In step 3, use a drained chunky salsa for the sauce, then top with 1 cup cooked beef mince or shredded cooked chicken, ½ cup corn kernels, and vegetables and cheese as above.

For the sauce, you can use bolognese, thick pasta sauce, chunky salsa or a thick vegetable puree such as pumpkin, sweet potato or carrot mash. If the sauce has excess liquid, drain in a fine-mesh sieve to remove, to prevent the scrolls from becoming soggy.

SWAP IT!
Change up the flavour by adding in your children's favourite ingredients – or even use the leftovers in the fridge.

SWAP IT!
Swap hummus for the avocado, if preferred. Use poached chicken breast or salmon instead of tuna.

Tuna Tabbouleh Wraps

PREP + COOK TIME 20 MINUTES (+ COOLING) **SERVES** 2

¼ cup (50g) quinoa
¾ cup (180ml) water
1 medium tomato (150g), seeded, chopped finely
1 green onion, chopped finely
2 tablespoons chopped fresh flat-leaf parsley
2 tablespoons chopped fresh mint
1 tablespoon olive oil
1½ tablespoons lemon juice
½ small avocado (100g), mashed (see Swap It)
2 wholemeal wraps (150g) (see Tip)
185g can tuna, drained, flaked (see Swap It)

1 Rinse and drain quinoa. Bring quinoa and the water to the boil in a small saucepan over high heat. Reduce heat to low; cook, covered, for 15 minutes or until liquid is absorbed. Cool.

2 To make tabbouleh, transfer quinoa to a medium bowl, then add tomato, onion, herbs, oil and juice; stir to combine. Season to taste.

3 Spread avocado over wraps, then top with tuna and tabbouleh. Roll up. Secure at two intervals with baking paper or paper, and kitchen string. Halve wraps.

SERVING SUGGESTIONS

The wraps can be toasted in a sandwich press. For adults, add a little chilli sauce, if you like, or use tuna in chilli oil.

For a gluten-free version, choose gluten-free wraps. To save time, you can buy tabbouleh; however, it won't be gluten-free.

After-School Snacks

DELICIOUS TREATS, GOOD FOR YOUR SOUL! DECORATE WITH SEA SALT, PISTACHIOS OR EDIBLE ROSE PETALS.

SALTED DATE CARAMELS

PREP + COOK TIME 20 MINUTES (+ STANDING & FREEZING) **MAKES** 15

- 2 cups (310g) fresh dates, pitted
- ¾ cup (150g) coconut oil
- ¼ cup (25g) cacao powder
- 1 teaspoon vanilla extract
- 2 tablespoons coconut oil, extra, at room temperature
- ½ teaspoon sea salt flakes
- ¼ cup (50g) coconut flour
- sea salt flakes, extra, for sprinkling

1 Place dates in a medium bowl. Cover with boiling water; stand for 10 minutes to soften. Drain dates; discard water.

2 Meanwhile, melt oil in a small saucepan; combine oil and sifted cacao in a small bowl. Stand until thickened slightly.

3 Process dates, vanilla, extra oil and salt until smooth. Transfer mixture to a small bowl; cover and freeze for 30 minutes or until firm.

4 Line an oven tray with baking paper. Place flour in a small bowl. Using damp hands, roll tablespoons of the date mixture into balls. Roll balls in coconut flour. Using a spoon, dip date balls into cacao coating, then place on tray. Sprinkle with extra salt. Freeze for 10 minutes or until set.

Don't worry if the coating on the caramels has a whitish look – this is simply the coconut oil and won't affect the taste. Place the caramels in small paper cases or wrap in coloured paper for a fun serving idea.

FOOD FACT!
Dates contain both soluble and insoluble fibre as well as different kinds of amino acids, making them good for your digestive system.

Bean Quesadillas

PREP + COOK TIME 15 MINUTES **SERVES** 4

- 400g can black beans, drained, rinsed
- 8 x 15cm mini flour tortillas (200g) (see Tip)
- 1 large tomato (220g), chopped finely
- 125g can corn kernels, drained
- 1 cup (120g) grated cheddar cheese (see Tip)

1 Preheat a sandwich press (see Tip).
2 Mash beans lightly in a bowl with the back of a fork.
3 Spread the mashed beans over 4 tortillas; top with tomato, corn and cheese. Place remaining tortillas on top.
4 Lightly oil sandwich press. Cook tortillas, in batches, in sandwich press for 1 minute or until browned on both sides and cheese is melted.
5 Cut quesadillas into wedges to serve.

SERVING SUGGESTIONS

Serve quesadillas with lime and sliced avocado. For adults, add hot chilli sauce and coriander.

For a gluten-free option, use corn tortillas or gluten-free wraps. For a dairy-free option, use grated vegan cheese. You can also cook the quesadillas in a frying pan or under a preheated grill, turning once, until they are browned on both sides.

GLUTEN-FREE SEED CRACKERS

PREP + COOK TIME 45 MINUTES (+ COOLING) **MAKES** 20

- 2 tablespoons chia seeds
- ½ cup (125ml) water
- 1 cup (150g) sunflower seeds
- ½ cup (100g) pepitas (pumpkin seed kernels)
- ½ cup (75g) buckwheat flour
- ¼ cup (40g) sesame seeds
- ¼ cup (50g) coconut oil, melted
- 1 teaspoon sea salt

1 Place a large oven tray in the oven and preheat oven to 180°C.

2 Combine chia seeds and the water in a small bowl; soak for 10 minutes until a thick gel forms.

3 Meanwhile, pulse sunflower seeds and pepitas in a food processor until finely chopped. Transfer to a large bowl; stir in flour and sesame seeds. Add chia gel, coconut oil and salt. Using hands, mix and shape into a ball.

4 Roll dough out between two sheets of baking paper to a 23cm x 33cm, 3mm thick rectangle. Score into assorted shapes or rectangles. Using the baking paper, lift dough onto preheated tray.

5 Bake for 25 minutes or until crisp and lightly brown. While still warm, cut following score marks; cool crackers completely on tray.

Store crackers in an airtight container for up to 4 days.

SERVING SUGGESTION

Serve crackers with nut spread, avocado or hummus and scatter with baby coriander or parsley.

FOOD FACT!
As well as being high in omega-3 fatty acids, chia seeds are rich in antioxidants and are a source of fibre, iron and calcium.

SWAP IT!
Any colourful fruit can be used as a 'pizza' topping, although fruit that browns when cut, such as apples, pears and bananas, should not be used unless the 'pizza' is served immediately.

Fruit 'Pizza' Wedges with 'Fries'

PREP TIME 10 MINUTES **SERVES** 4

20cm diameter round seedless watermelon slice with rind, cut 2cm thick
1 kiwifruit, peeled, sliced
4 strawberries, hulled, sliced crossways
14 blueberries
100g piece fresh pineapple, peeled, cut into matchsticks
100g piece tasty or colby cheese (not crumbly)

1 Place watermelon on a board. Cut into eight wedges. Transfer to a plate.
2 Top watermelon with kiwifruit and berries, then pineapple to resemble shredded cheese on a pizza.
3 Cut cheese into 'fries', about 1cm thick. Serve fruit 'pizza' with cheese 'fries' on the side.

The pizza can be assembled up to 3 hours ahead; store in the fridge.

GREEN MACHINE

PREP TIME 5 MINUTES SERVES 2

1 medium lime (90g) (optional) (see Tip)
1 medium green apple (150g)
1 Lebanese cucumber (130g)
½ medium avocado (125g)
1¼ cups (310ml) coconut water (see Swap It)
80g baby spinach leaves

1 Remove rind with pith from lime; discard. Coarsely chop lime flesh, apple, cucumber and avocado.

2 Blend or process lime, apple, cucumber and avocado in a high-powered blender with coconut water and spinach until smooth. Divide between two glasses; serve immediately.

SERVING SUGGESTION

You can top the smoothies with toasted coconut and white or black chia seeds, if you like.

You might like to leave the lime out for young children, or squeeze the juice and add it gradually to the finished smoothie. This smoothie is dairy-free.

SWAP IT!
Use a variety of green vegetables or fruits, such as lettuce, pear or honeydew melon. Prefer a sweeter juice? Swap the coconut water with fresh juice.

SWAP IT!
Vary the fruit according to your taste and what's in season; use the same quantities.

BERRY FROYO

I KEEP THESE FRUITY CUBES IN THE FREEZER FOR AN AFTER-SCHOOL SNACK READY IN MINUTES.

PREP TIME 10 MINUTES (+ FREEZING) **SERVES** 4

1½ cups (420g) Greek-style yoghurt
1 tablespoon honey
200g coarsely chopped pineapple
250g strawberries, halved
250g fresh mixed berries

1 Blend yoghurt, honey, pineapple and strawberries until smooth. Pour mixture into four 12-hole ice-cube trays (1-tablespoon capacity). Freeze for 4 hours or until frozen.

2 Serve froyo berry cubes with fresh mixed berries and topped with mint, if you like.

The froyo cubes will soften into a slushy-style drink. I often blitz and freeze leftover or overripe fruit in ice-cube trays, as they are perfect for these snacks; they also add colour and fun to drinking water.

PACKED WITH HEALTHY FATS FROM THE NUTS, THE TASTE KEEPS KIDS COMING BACK FOR MORE!

AMAZE BALLS

PREP + COOK TIME 10 MINUTES MAKES 16

- ½ cup (80g) sultanas
- ¼ cup (40g) almonds (see Tip)
- 1 tablespoon coconut oil, melted
- 1 tablespoon honey
- 1 teaspoon cacao powder
- ½ cup (40g) shredded coconut
- 1 tablespoon chocolate protein powder (10g)
- ½ cup (40g) desiccated coconut

1 Place all ingredients, except desiccated coconut, into a food processor. Process for 30 seconds or until the mixture comes together. You will need to watch closely as it goes from being a dry mixture to being too soft very quickly (the sultanas are where the moisture comes from).

2 Roll 3 level teaspoons of mixture into balls. Roll balls in desiccated coconut. Refrigerate on a tray until firm. Transfer to an airtight container; keep refrigerated.

For a nut-free version for school lunchboxes, use a mixture of seeds and desiccated coconut in place of the almonds. Keep balls in an airtight container in the fridge for up to 1 month or freeze for up to 3 months.

Coconut & mango pops

PREP + COOK TIME 25 MINUTES (+ FREEZING) MAKES 8

- 1¾ cups (265g) frozen diced mango
- ½ cup (125ml) pure fresh apple juice (see Tip)
- 2 tablespoons Natvia (see Tip)
- 400ml can coconut cream
- ½ teaspoon sea salt flakes
- ¼ cup (10g) shredded coconut, toasted (optional)

1 Process mango and apple juice until smooth. Place 2 tablespoons mango puree into each of eight ½-cup (125ml) popsicle moulds; freeze for 30 minutes.

2 Whisk Natvia, coconut cream and salt in a medium bowl until Natvia is dissolved. Spoon mixture into popsicle moulds to fill. Cover moulds with a double layer of plastic wrap (this will help to keep the popsicle sticks upright). Pierce the plastic with a small knife, then push popsicle sticks into each hole. Freeze for at least 4 hours or overnight.

3 Place toasted coconut in a small bowl. Dip popsicle moulds briefly in boiling water to remove popsicles. Dip each popsicle quickly in hot water then into the coconut. Freeze on a baking-paper-lined tray for 10 minutes or until ready to eat.

You can juice apples in a juice extractor or buy unsweetened chilled apple juice. Natvia is a 100% natural sweetener made with organic stevia; it has minimal effect on blood glucose levels.

Choc-cranberry snack bars

PREP + COOK TIME 50 MINUTES (+ COOLING) **MAKES** 16 BARS

2½ cups (50g) puffed millet or rice
½ cup (60g) pecan nuts, chopped (see Swap It)
⅓ cup (65g) pepitas (pumpkin seed kernels)
¼ cup (35g) dried unsweetened cranberries, chopped coarsely
2 tablespoons LSA (see Tip)
1 tablespoon sesame seeds
½ cup (180g) honey (see Tip)
1 teaspoon vanilla extract
½ teaspoon salt flakes
45g sugar-free dark chocolate, chopped coarsely

1 Preheat oven to 150°C. Grease a 20cm square cake pan; line base and two opposite sides with baking paper, extending the paper 5cm over sides.

2 Combine puffed millet, pecans, pepitas, cranberries, LSA and sesame seeds in a large bowl.

3 Place honey, vanilla and salt in a small saucepan over medium heat; cook, stirring, for 2 minutes or until mixture just comes to a simmer. Pour honey mixture over dry ingredients; stir through until evenly coated. Cool for 5 minutes. Add chocolate; stir until combined. Transfer mixture to pan; press down firmly with the back of a spoon.

4 Bake for 30 minutes or until golden brown. Cool in pan. Cut into 16 bars.

LSA is a ground mixture of linseeds, sunflower seeds and almonds. It is available from supermarkets and health food stores. When measuring honey, lightly spray the measuring cup with oil first and the honey will slide out more easily.

SWAP IT!
For a nut-free version, swap pecans for the same amount of chopped dried fruit.

Weeknights Fast!

A FAST WEEKNIGHT DINNER, PACKED WITH PROTEIN AND ALL THE RIGHT INGREDIENTS TO HELP YOUR KIDS GROW!

Warm Chicken & Rice Salad

PREP + COOK TIME 10 MINUTES **SERVES** 4

- 450g packet cooked brown rice (see Swap It)
- 2 cups (320g) cooked shredded chicken breast
- ½ cup (80g) chopped dry roasted almonds
- 4 green onions, sliced thinly
- 1 small red capsicum (150g), chopped
- 2 tablespoons coconut oil, melted
- ½ teaspoon paprika
- ½ teaspoon organic ground cinnamon
- 1 teaspoon Himalayan salt

1 Heat rice in a large microwave-safe bowl for 2 minutes on HIGH (100%). Add chicken, almonds, onion and capsicum to the bowl; mix well.

2 Stir through the combined coconut oil and spices before serving. Season to taste with salt. Sprinkle with extra sliced green onion, if you like.

SWAP IT!

You can swap the brown rice for another pre-cooked rice or rice mix, such as brown basmati, or brown rice and quinoa.

FOOD FACT!
There's a reason we should eat our greens – they're nutritional powerhouses packed with fibre, folate and vitamins A, C and K – and they add colour to this dish!

HULK Pasta

PREP + COOK TIME 15 MINUTES SERVES 4

- 1 tablespoon olive oil
- 1 medium onion (150g), chopped finely
- 2 cloves garlic, crushed
- ½ teaspoon paprika
- 2 small zucchini (180g), chopped coarsely
- 100g broccoli, chopped coarsely
- 50g baby spinach
- 2 teaspoons lemon juice
- 400g packet fettuccine-style slim pasta (organic konjac), drained (see Tip)
- parmesan flakes, to serve (optional)

1 Heat the oil in a medium saucepan over medium heat. Cook onion, garlic, paprika, zucchini and broccoli, stirring, for 5 minutes or until vegetables are just tender. Add the spinach; cook, stirring, until wilted. Stir in the lemon juice. Blend or process vegetable mixture until smooth. Add salt and pepper to taste.

2 Heat the pasta following packet directions.

3 Toss the sauce and pasta together in a bowl. Serve with parmesan, if you like.

SERVING SUGGESTION

For adults, try adding spices or fresh chilli in step 3.

Slim pasta is made from a vegetable called konjac, which has been consumed in Asian countries for centuries. Konjac is low in calories and carbohydrates.

SUNSHINE IN A BOWL

PREP + COOK TIME 35 MINUTES (+ STANDING) SERVES 4

- 2 teaspoons coconut oil
- 2 large leeks (1kg), sliced thinly
- ½ teaspoon finely grated fresh ginger
- 1 teaspoon curry powder
- 2 medium orange sweet potatoes (600g), chopped
- 1 litre (4 cups) water
- ⅓ cup (100g) Greek-style yoghurt
- 2 tablespoons chopped fresh chives

1 Heat the oil in a large saucepan; cook leeks, stirring occasionally, for 5 minutes or until soft. Add the ginger and curry powder; stir to combine.

2 Add the sweet potato and the water. Bring to the boil; reduce heat and simmer for 20 minutes. Remove from the heat; stand for 10 minutes.

3 Blend or process soup mixture until smooth. Season to taste. Return soup to pan; stir over low heat until hot.

4 Serve soup topped with yoghurt, chives and a little freshly ground pepper, if you like.

FOOD FACT!

Sweet potatoes are an excellent source of beta-carotene, which the body transforms into vitamin A, essential for healthy eyes.

FOOD FACT!
Tuna is a great source of lean protein and is packed to the gills with B vitamins, which help convert food into fuel to keep you energised.

Tuna Pasta with Pesto & Tomatoes

PREP + COOK TIME 25 MINUTES SERVES 4

300g spaghetti
2 tablespoons olive oil
2 cloves garlic, sliced thinly
400g cherry tomatoes
185g can tuna in oil, drained, flaked
⅓ cup fresh basil leaves
1 medium lemon (140g), cut into wedges

PESTO

⅔ cup fresh basil leaves
⅓ cup (25g) finely grated parmesan
1½ tablespoons pine nuts
1 clove garlic, crushed
⅓ cup (80ml) olive oil

1 Cook pasta in a large saucepan of boiling water, following packet directions, until tender.
2 Meanwhile, make pesto.
3 Reserve ¼ cup of cooking water, then drain pasta.
4 Heat a large non-stick frying pan over medium heat. Add oil and garlic; cook for 30 seconds or until fragrant. Add tomatoes; cook for 2 minutes or until blistered.
5 Add pasta to pan with reserved cooking water and tuna. Increase heat to high; cook, stirring, for 2 minutes or until hot. Stir in pesto; season to taste.
6 Sprinkle pasta with basil leaves; serve with lemon wedges.
pesto Blend or process ingredients until smooth.

SERVING SUGGESTION

For adults, try adding 2 fresh long red chillies, seeded and chopped, to the pan in step 4.

You can make the pesto a day ahead and store, covered, in the fridge.

WHO DOESN'T LOVE A BURGER? SWAP THE TAKEOUT FOR HOMEMADE AND YOU HAVE A FAMILY MEAL PACKED WITH NUTRIENTS.

MEGA BURGERS

PREP + COOK TIME 25 MINUTES **MAKES** 4

- 1 tablespoon olive oil
- 1 medium red onion (170g), sliced
- 400g beef mince (see Tip)
- 125g sliced cheddar
- 4 eggs
- 4 burger buns, split, or 1 loaf Turkish bread, cut into quarters and split
- ¼ cup (75g) aioli or mayonnaise
- 4 butter or iceberg lettuce leaves
- ⅓ cup (110g) relish, or sauce of your choice
- 1 large tomato (220g), sliced thickly
- ⅓ cup (120g) sliced pickled dill cucumber

1 Preheat a barbecue plate or frying pan over medium heat. Add oil and onion; cook for 5 minutes or until onion softens. Push onion to a cooler part of the barbecue to keep warm.

2 Meanwhile, season mince well; shape into four patties. Increase barbecue heat to high. Cook patties for 2 minutes each side or until just cooked through. Top with cheddar while hot. Transfer to a plate; keep warm. Crack eggs on barbecue; cook until egg whites are set, edges are crisp and yolks are cooked to your liking. Transfer to a plate; keep warm. Toast buns, cut-side down, on barbecue for 1 minute.

3 To assemble burgers, spread bun bases with aioli. Top with lettuce, patties, relish, eggs, tomato, pickles, onion, then the bun tops.

The minced meat for the patties should not be too lean for the best results. Cook 200g sliced mushrooms with the onion, if you like.

SWAP IT!
Replace beef with chicken, lamb or prawns.

Peanut-free Satay Beef Skewers

PREP + COOK TIME 30 MINUTES SERVES 4–6

⅓ cup (95g) nut-free butter (see Tip)
270ml can coconut milk
2 tablespoons soy sauce or tamari
1 tablespoon mild chilli sauce
1 tablespoon honey
2 tablespoons lime juice
750g beef rump steak, fat trimmed (see Swap It)
2 tablespoons soy sauce or tamari, extra
2 teaspoons honey, extra
1 green onion, sliced thinly lengthways
200g snow peas, trimmed, sliced
2 cups (300g) cooked jasmine rice
2 tablespoons fresh coriander leaves

Nut-free butter is made from sunflower seeds; it is available from health food stores. Satay sauce can be made a day ahead; store in an airtight container in the fridge. Reheat before serving.

1 To make satay sauce, heat a small heavy-based saucepan over medium heat; cook butter and coconut milk, without boiling, stirring until smooth. Stir in sauces, honey and juice; cook, stirring, for 1 minute or until hot.

2 Cut steak into long thin strips. Thread steak onto 12 bamboo skewers. Cook skewers on a heated oiled grill pan (or grill or barbecue) for 2 minutes each side or until cooked as desired, brushing with combined extra soy sauce and honey in the final 2 minutes of cooking.

3 Meanwhile, place green onion in a bowl of cold water to curl. Steam or microwave snow peas until just tender.

4 Serve skewers with rice, snow peas and satay sauce; scatter with coriander and green onion.

SERVING SUGGESTION

Serve skewers with stir-fried vegetables.

Chicken Crunch Stir-fry

PREP + COOK TIME 35 MINUTES (+ STANDING & COOLING) SERVES 4

- 2 tablespoons light soy sauce
- 1 tablespoon honey
- 600g chicken breast fillets, sliced thinly
- ¼ cup (50g) coconut oil
- 2 medium carrots (240g), cut into matchsticks
- 200g snow peas, halved lengthways
- 2 cloves garlic, sliced thinly
- 4 green onions, sliced thinly
- ¼ teaspoon sesame oil

TAMARI ALMOND CRUNCH

- ¼ cup (40g) tamari almonds
- 1½ tablespoons sesame seeds

1 Combine 1 tablespoon of the soy sauce with honey in a medium bowl; add chicken. Toss chicken to coat in marinade; stand for 10 minutes.

2 Meanwhile, make tamari almond crunch.

3 Heat 1 tablespoon of the coconut oil in a wok or large heavy-based frying pan over high heat. Stir-fry chicken, in batches, using another 1 tablespoon of the oil, for 3 minutes or until browned and cooked through. Transfer to a bowl.

4 Add remaining oil to wok; add carrot, snow peas, garlic and onion. Stir-fry for 2 minutes or until snow peas are bright green and just tender. Return chicken to wok with sesame oil and remaining soy sauce; stir to combine.

5 Sprinkle chicken mixture with tamari almond crunch; serve.

tamari almond crunch Place almonds and sesame seeds in a dry heavy-based frying pan over medium heat. Cook, shaking the pan, for 2 minutes or until sesame seeds are golden. Transfer to a board; cool. Chop almond mixture coarsely.

SERVING SUGGESTIONS

Serve with steamed rice and extra sliced green onion. For adults, serve with Sriracha, a Thai-style chilli sauce available from selected supermarkets and Asian food stores, or substitute with whatever chilli sauce you have on hand, or add a little fresh seeded chilli.

You can marinate the chicken in a covered bowl in the fridge for 2 hours or overnight.

SWAP IT!
Swap the yoghurt for whole-egg mayonnaise, if you prefer.

Baked Fish 'n' Chips

PREP + COOK TIME 40 MINUTES SERVES 4–6

4 small orange sweet potatoes (1kg), unpeeled, cut into thin wedges
1 tablespoon olive oil
1 teaspoon sweet paprika
¼ cup (40g) sesame seeds
1 cup (75g) panko (Japanese) breadcrumbs
¼ cup (35g) plain flour
2 eggs
800g skinless boneless firm white fish fillets (see Tip)
olive oil cooking spray
1 green onion, sliced thinly lengthways
1 lemon, cut into wedges

YOGHURT TARTARE
2 baby gherkins (30g), chopped finely
2 green onions, chopped finely
1 tablespoon chopped dill
½ cup (140g) Greek-style yoghurt (see Swap It)

1 Preheat oven to 220°C. Line two oven trays with baking paper.
2 Combine sweet potato and oil in a medium bowl; season. Place sweet potato, in a single layer, on one tray; roast for 20 minutes.
3 Meanwhile, combine paprika, seeds and breadcrumbs in a shallow bowl. Place flour in another shallow bowl. Lightly beat eggs in another shallow bowl. Coat fish in flour; shake off any excess. Dip fish in egg, then in breadcrumb mixture, turning until fish is completely covered.
4 Place fish on second oven tray. Spray lightly with olive oil on both sides. Bake fish on a separate shelf to chips for 5 minutes. Turn the fish and chips; roast for a further 5 minutes or until the fish and chips are browned, crisp and cooked through.
5 Meanwhile, place green onion in a bowl of cold water to curl; stand for 5 minutes. Make yoghurt tartare.
6 Serve fish with chips, tartare, onion and lemon wedges.
yoghurt tartare Combine ingredients in a small bowl; season to taste.

I used flathead fillets here, but you could use ling, snapper, whiting or blue-eye trevalla.

Moroccan Lamb with Couscous

PREP + COOK TIME 25 MINUTES SERVES 4

- 2 teaspoons Moroccan seasoning
- 2 tablespoons olive oil
- 12 French-trimmed lamb cutlets (600g)
- 1 medium yellow capsicum (200g)
- 1 medium red capsicum (200g)
- 2 cups (500ml) water
- 30g butter
- 1 teaspoon sea salt flakes
- 2 cups (400g) couscous
- ¼ cup torn fresh mint leaves
- 200g hummus

1 Preheat grill.

2 Combine seasoning and half the oil in a large bowl; add lamb and turn to coat in mixture.

3 Quarter capsicums; discard seeds and membranes. Place, skin-side up, on a foil-lined oven tray; drizzle with remaining oil. Place under hot grill for 10 minutes or until skin blisters and blackens. Cover capsicum with plastic wrap or paper and leave for 5 minutes; peel away skin, then slice thinly.

4 Meanwhile, bring the water, butter and salt to the boil in a medium saucepan. Stir in couscous; cover and remove from heat. Stand for 5 minutes. Fluff with a fork. Place couscous and capsicum in a large bowl with mint; toss to combine.

5 Cook lamb on a heated grill plate (or grill or barbecue) over medium-high heat for 4 minutes each side or until cooked as desired.

6 Serve lamb with couscous salad and hummus.

To save time, use store-bought roasted capsicum, available from the deli or in jars.

SERVING SUGGESTION

Serve with a tomato and cucumber salad.

FOOD FACT!
Capsicums are a rich source of vitamins A and C, which are both powerful antioxidants that help fight free radicals in the body.

FOOD FACT!
Spinach is loaded with good things for every part of your body – niacin, zinc, protein, fibre and vitamins A, C, E and K, to name a few.

Tandoori lamb wraps

PREP + COOK TIME 40 MINUTES (+ REFRIGERATION) **SERVES** 4

1 tablespoon tandoori paste
1 tablespoon Greek-style yoghurt
600g lamb backstraps (eye of loin)
2 Lebanese cucumbers (260g), seeded, sliced
250g grape tomatoes, halved
6 red radishes (90g), sliced
1 tablespoon white balsamic vinegar
60g baby spinach leaves

GREEN ONION WRAPS

1 cup (150g) self-raising flour
½ cup (140g) Greek-style yoghurt
1 green onion, sliced thinly
2 tablespoons coconut oil

1 Combine paste and yoghurt in a large bowl; add lamb and turn to coat. Cook lamb in a heated oiled frying pan over medium-high heat for about 8 minutes or until browned all over and cooked as desired. Transfer to a plate; cover with foil. Stand for 10 minutes.

2 Meanwhile, make green onion wraps.

3 Combine cucumber with tomato, radish and vinegar in a medium bowl; season with salt. Stand for 5 minutes.

4 Slice lamb thinly. Serve lamb, spinach and salad in wraps.

green onion wraps Place flour, yoghurt and onion in a bowl; stir with a butter knife until combined. Knead gently on a lightly floured surface until dough is smooth. Divide dough into eight balls. Lightly flour work surface with extra flour. Using a rolling pin, roll each ball into an 18cm round. Melt 1 teaspoon of the oil in a heated small frying pan over high heat. Cook one of the wraps for 1 minute each side or until browned. Transfer to a plate; cover with foil to keep warm. Repeat with the remaining oil and dough to make eight wraps in total; stack wraps to keep them soft and warm.

SERVING SUGGESTION

Serve with extra yoghurt, if you like.

Dough can be made 8 hours ahead; store, covered, in the fridge. Stand at room temperature for 20 minutes before cooking.

ONE-POT MAC 'N' CHEESE

PREP + COOK TIME 20 MINUTES SERVES 4

1 litre (4 cups) water
3 cups (400g) macaroni or elbow macaroni
1 teaspoon salt
40g butter, chopped
2 cups (240g) grated cheddar (see Swap It)
¾ cup (60g) grated parmesan (see Swap It)
½ cup (140g) Greek-style yoghurt
1 teaspoon Dijon mustard (optional)

1 Place the water, macaroni, salt and butter in a medium saucepan over medium heat. Cook, stirring, until mixture comes to the boil. Reduce heat to low-medium; cook, stirring continuously, for 8 minutes or until pasta is just cooked through and liquid is thickened and reduced (the butter and starch from the pasta will thicken the pasta cooking water). If the pasta starts to catch in the corner or the mixture becomes too dry before cooking through, add a few tablespoons of extra water.

2 Stir in cheeses and yoghurt until cheese melts. Stir in mustard. Season to taste; serve.

GREEN MAC 'N' CHEESE (PICTURED)

Stir in 1 cup frozen peas in step 2 and 100g baby spinach leaves at the end to wilt.

TUNA MAC 'N' CHEESE

Stir in a drained 425g can tuna at the end to heat through.

CHICKEN & MUSHROOM MAC 'N' CHEESE

Before starting the recipe, cook 200g sliced mushrooms in a little oil or butter in the pan until browned lightly; remove from pan. Stir the mushrooms and 1 cup shredded cooked chicken in at the end to heat through.

SWAP IT!
Use any cheeses you have on hand. Replace some of the cheddar with blue cheese, feta, brie, gouda, Swiss or gruyère.

"A healthy outside starts from the inside!"

BEEF NOODLES WITH SESAME

PREP + COOK TIME 25 MINUTES SERVES 4

400g beef rump steak, sliced thinly
2 teaspoons soy sauce or tamari
2 teaspoons sesame oil
200g soba noodles
1 tablespoon coconut oil
250g broccoli, cut into florets
1 small red capsicum (150g), sliced
4 green onions, cut into lengths, green tops sliced thinly for serving

CREAMY SESAME DRESSING

2 tablespoons rice wine vinegar
2 tablespoons water
1 tablespoon soy sauce or tamari
1 tablespoon natural crunchy peanut butter (see Tip)
1 tablespoon pure maple syrup
2 teaspoons tahini
2 teaspoons sesame oil

For nut allergies, use a nut-free butter, available from health food stores.

1 Toss beef with combined soy sauce and 1 teaspoon of the sesame oil.
2 Make creamy sesame dressing.
3 Cook noodles in a large saucepan of boiling water, following packet directions. Rinse under cold running water; drain.
4 Heat a large wok over high heat. Add half the coconut oil and the remaining sesame oil; stir-fry beef, in batches, for 2 minutes or until browned all over. Transfer to a large bowl. Add remaining coconut oil; stir-fry vegetables for 2 minutes or until just tender.
5 Return beef to wok with noodles and vegetables. Add creamy sesame dressing; toss well.
6 Divide noodle mixture among bowls. Sprinkle with sliced green onion tops.

creamy sesame dressing Place ingredients in a small bowl; whisk until smooth. Makes ⅔ cup.

SERVING SUGGESTION

For adults, serve with chilli sauce.

Prawn Zoodle Pad Thai

PREP + COOK TIME 30 MINUTES SERVES 4

- 2 fresh seeded dates (40g), chopped
- ⅔ cup (100g) roasted cashews, 1 tablespoon reserved
- ⅔ cup (160ml) water
- 2 tablespoons lime juice
- 1 tablespoon coarsely chopped fresh ginger
- 2 cloves garlic, crushed
- ½ bunch fresh coriander, roots and stems washed and chopped finely, leaves picked
- 1 large zucchini (150g)
- 150g mung bean vermicelli
- 1 tablespoon olive oil
- 800g uncooked king prawns, peeled, deveined, with tails intact
- 2 medium carrots (240g), cut into matchsticks
- 1 lime (65g), cut into wedges

1 Process dates, cashews, the water, juice, ginger, garlic, and coriander roots and stems in a small food processor until mixture forms a smooth paste.

2 Using a vegetable spiraliser, cut zucchini into spirals (see Tip). Drop zucchini noodles in a saucepan of boiling water; drain immediately and rinse under cold running water.

3 Cook vermicelli until tender, following packet directions; drain.

4 Heat oil in a large wok or heavy-based frying pan over high heat. Add prawns and carrot; stir-fry for 2 minutes or until just cooked through. Add cashew paste; stir to combine and warm through.

5 Add vermicelli and zucchini to wok; stir-fry for 1 minute or until heated through. Season to taste with pepper.

6 Top the pad Thai with some of the coriander leaves and the reserved cashews; serve with lime wedges.

If you have a vegetable spiraliser, making vegetable noodles is a cinch. If not, slice the zucchini using a julienne peeler, mandoline or V-slicer. You can also grate the zucchini on the coarse side of a box grater.

SWAP IT!
Use boneless and skinless fish fillets in place of the chicken, if you like.

Chicken & Corn Tacos

PREP + COOK TIME 35 MINUTES SERVES 4

- 2 trimmed corn cobs (500g)
- olive oil cooking spray
- 500g chicken tenderloins (see Swap It)
- 1 teaspoon Mexican chilli powder (see Tip)
- 1 medium red capsicum (200g), chopped finely
- ½ medium avocado (125g), chopped
- 4 green onions, sliced
- 2 tablespoons lime juice
- 2 tablespoons chopped fresh coriander
- 4 wholegrain tortillas (160g)
- 1 lime (65g), cut into wedges

1 Spray corn with oil; cook on a heated grill plate (or barbecue) over high heat, turning occasionally, for 10 minutes or until charred and tender. Cool.

2 Sprinkle chicken with chilli powder; grill for 4 minutes each side or until cooked through. Cover loosely with foil; rest for 10 minutes, then slice in half diagonally.

3 When corn is cool enough to handle, cut kernels from cobs, in sections if possible.

4 To make salsa, place capsicum, avocado, onion, juice and half the coriander in a bowl; stir gently to combine.

5 Place tortillas on a heated oiled grill plate (or barbecue) for 30 seconds each side or until golden and grill marks appear. Transfer to a plate; cover with a clean tea towel to prevent drying out.

6 Fill tacos evenly with salsa and chicken; top with corn and remaining coriander. Serve with lime wedges.

You can reduce the amount of Mexican chilli powder, or use Mexican seasoning instead.

Sticky Chicken with Slaw

PREP + COOK TIME 30 MINUTES (+ REFRIGERATION) **SERVES** 4–6

- 750g chicken tenderloins or breast fillets
- 1 teaspoon Chinese five-spice powder
- 2 cloves garlic, crushed
- 2 tablespoons coconut oil
- 2 tablespoons lime juice
- ¼ cup (60ml) fish sauce
- ¼ cup (90g) honey
- ½ cup (125ml) water
- 1 fresh long red chilli, seeded, sliced thinly (optional) (see Tip)
- 170g wombok (Chinese cabbage), shredded finely
- 2 green onions, sliced thinly
- 1 cup firmly packed fresh coriander leaves
- 1 large green-skinned apple (200g), cut into matchsticks

1 Combine chicken with five-spice, garlic and oil. Refrigerate for 1 hour. Thread chicken onto eight skewers.

2 To make dressing, place juice, 1 tablespoon fish sauce and 1 tablespoon honey in a screw-top jar; shake well.

3 To make caramel, combine remaining honey and the water in a small saucepan over low heat; add chilli. Bring to the boil over medium heat. Boil, without stirring, for 4 minutes or until the syrup reduces by half. Add remaining fish sauce; simmer for 5 minutes or until thickened and syrupy. Cool slightly.

4 Cook skewers on a heated grill plate (or grill or barbecue) over medium-high heat for 4 minutes each side, turning occasionally, or until cooked through. Transfer to a warm plate.

5 To make the slaw, place wombok, onion, coriander and apple in a large bowl. Drizzle with dressing; toss gently to combine.

6 Drizzle chicken skewers with caramel; serve with slaw.

Long chillies are usually not too hot, especially when the seeds are removed. Caramel can be made 3 days ahead; store, covered, in the fridge.

Do-ahead Dinners

IF YOU'RE A BUSY PARENT (CUE EVERYONE RAISING THEIR HANDS), GETTING DINNER ON THE TABLE AT A REASONABLE TIME IS A MISSION! A FEW KEY THINGS I LIKE TO DO TO HELP WITH THE NIGHTLY MAYHEM ARE TO PLAN THE WEEK OUT IN ADVANCE AND PREP ANYTHING I CAN ON SUNDAY, BEFORE THE WEEK KICK-STARTS. SHOPPING TO A WEEKLY MENU ALSO ENSURES WE STICK TO OUR BUDGET.

PREPARATION IS KEY!

GREAT FOOD PREP STARTS AT THE SUPERMARKET.

Sunday is our meal-prep day. The boys love being involved in the kitchen, and it's awesome that I can now give them a recipe and they can make it, whether it's a meal or baked goodies. I find they enjoy cooking things they genuinely love, so I find recipes they want to create, which makes cooking fun and not a chore.

AS PARENTS, WE MUST TAKE RESPONSIBILITY FOR THE FOOD CHOICES OUR CHILDREN MAKE. IF THERE ARE ONLY GREAT, HEALTHY CHOICES IN THE FRIDGE AND PANTRY, THEY CAN ONLY SELECT GREAT, HEALTHY OPTIONS.

I ALWAYS have fruit cut up in the fridge (watermelon and rockmelon) and a large fruit bowl fully stocked. I keep 100g servings of cooked chicken breast stored in containers in the fridge so I can make a quick snack for the girls, or if the boys want something more filling, they can easily make a wrap without much fuss.

Make double batches where possible – twice the reward for half the effort! Individually portioned baked goods freeze well for lunchboxes. Recipes like quiche or zucchini fritters do double-duty as lunch and dinner. Pasta sauces can be portioned and frozen for a quick meal, and not just for pasta – top jacket potatoes, sweet potatoes, steamed greens, or even zoodles, with pasta sauces.

TO HELP EASE THE MORNING RUSH, I PREPARE THE KIDS' LUNCHES THE NIGHT BEFORE, TO GRAB-AND-GO AS WE RACE OUT THE DOOR.

BEEF CURRY WITH COCONUT SAMBAL

PREP + COOK TIME 3 HOURS SERVES 4–6

3 shallots (75g), chopped coarsely
5 cloves garlic, chopped coarsely
1 fresh long red chilli (optional)
30g piece fresh ginger, chopped finely
1 lemongrass stalk, white part only, sliced thinly
1 tablespoon coconut oil
1kg lean beef chuck steak, cut into 3cm pieces
1.5 litres (6 cups) water, approximately
½ cup (140g) Greek-style yoghurt
steamed rice and coriander, to serve

COCONUT SAMBAL

¼ cup (10g) flaked coconut, toasted
1 Lebanese cucumber (130g), seeded, chopped finely
½ small red onion (50g), chopped finely
1 tablespoon lime juice

1 To make rendang paste, process shallots, garlic, chilli, ginger and lemongrass until smooth.
2 Heat coconut oil in a large heavy-based saucepan over medium heat. Add paste; cook, stirring, for 3 minutes or until fragrant.
3 Add beef to pan with enough of the water to completely cover beef; bring to the boil. Reduce heat; simmer, uncovered, for 2½ hours (liquid will slowly evaporate and beef will become very tender). Add more water during cooking, if necessary.
4 Make coconut sambal.
5 Spoon yoghurt onto curry; serve with coconut sambal, steamed rice and coriander.
coconut sambal Combine ingredients in a small bowl.

To save time, buy ready-made rendang paste, available from the Asian section of most supermarkets.

IF YOUR CHILDREN ARE FUSSY EATERS, USE A GRATER OR FOOD PROCESSOR TO BLEND VEGETABLES INTO MEALS SUCH AS LASAGNE, FRITTATAS, SPAGHETTI AND PASTA SAUCES.

EGGPLANT LASAGNE

PREP + COOK TIME 1 HOUR 25 MINUTES **SERVES** 4

- 1 tablespoon coconut oil
- 1 medium onion (150g), chopped finely
- 2 cloves garlic, crushed
- 1 medium carrot (120g), grated coarsely
- 1 teaspoon ground cinnamon
- 1 teaspoon paprika
- 1 teaspoon Natvia
- 2 pinches Himalayan salt
- ¼ cup (60ml) water
- ¼ cup fresh basil leaves, chopped
- ¼ cup (70g) tomato paste
- 400g can red kidney beans, drained, rinsed
- 2 cups (500ml) tomato puree or bottled tomato passata
- 2 medium eggplants (700g), cut lengthways into 5mm-thick slices

1 Preheat the oven to 180°C.

2 Heat oil in a medium frying pan over medium heat. Cook onion and garlic, stirring, for 5 minutes or until softened. Add carrot, cinnamon, paprika, Natvia, salt and the water; cook, stirring, for 2 minutes or until carrot is softened. Stir in basil, tomato paste, kidney beans and tomato puree; simmer for 1 minute. Season to taste.

3 Lightly oil a 2.5-litre (10-cup) ovenproof dish. Place a quarter of the eggplant slices over the base of the dish; top with a quarter of the sauce. Repeat layering. Cover dish; bake lasagne for 1 hour or until eggplant is tender. Stand for 5 minutes before serving. Serve sprinkled with extra basil leaves, if you like.

This lasagne can be frozen for 2 months. Thaw in the fridge overnight; reheat, covered with foil, in the oven until hot.

DID YOU KNOW?

In Italian, 'lasagna' is the singular, while 'lasagne' is the plural, meaning more than one sheet of pasta.

Osso Buco

PREP + COOK TIME 2 HOURS 45 MINUTES **SERVES** 8

2kg veal osso buco
½ cup (75g) plain flour
2 tablespoons olive oil
2 medium onions (300g), chopped finely
2 cloves garlic, crushed
700g bottled tomato passata
2 cups (500ml) chicken stock
2 tablespoons fresh parsley leaves
lemon zest, to serve (optional)

SOFT POLENTA

2 cups (500ml) chicken stock
2 cups (500ml) milk
1 cup (170g) polenta
30g butter, chopped
½ cup (40g) grated parmesan

1 Preheat oven to 170°C.
2 Coat veal in flour; shake off excess. Heat oil in a large flameproof casserole dish over high heat; cook veal, in batches, for 2 minutes each side or until browned. Remove from pan.
3 Cook onion in same dish, stirring, over medium-high heat for 5 minutes or until softened. Add garlic; cook for 1 minute. Add passata and stock; return veal to pan. Spoon sauce mixture over veal; bring to the boil. Cover with a lid or foil. Cook in oven for 2 hours or until the veal is almost falling off the bone. Season to taste.
4 Meanwhile, make soft polenta.
5 Serve osso buco and soft polenta scattered with parsley and lemon zest.

soft polenta Bring stock and milk to the boil in a large deep saucepan. Add polenta in a thin steady stream and whisk until mixture comes to the boil. Reduce heat to low; cook, stirring with a long-handled wooden spoon or whisk, for 20 minutes until soft and thick. Stir in butter and parmesan. Season to taste. Adjust consistency with a little extra milk, if needed. Serve immediately.

SERVING SUGGESTIONS

Serve with mashed potato or rice instead of the polenta. Add a side of steamed green vegetables, such as beans, asparagus or peas, or a garden salad.

Osso buco can be frozen for up to 3 months; thaw in the fridge overnight before reheating.

Chicken & corn enchilada bake

PREP + COOK TIME 45 MINUTES **SERVES** 4

2 trimmed corn cobs (500g)
2 tablespoons olive oil
500g chicken breast fillets, sliced thinly (see Swap It)
1 medium red onion (170g), chopped finely
2 cloves garlic, crushed
1 fresh long green chilli, chopped (optional)
3 teaspoons smoked paprika
1½ teaspoons ground cumin
800g can diced tomatoes
1 tablespoon lime juice
8 x 20cm flour tortillas
2 cups (240g) coarsely grated cheddar
¼ cup fresh coriander sprigs
lime wedges, to serve

1 Preheat oven to 200°C.
2 Brush corn with 1 tablespoon of the oil. Heat a grill plate (or pan or barbecue) to medium-high heat; cook corn, turning occasionally, for 10 minutes or until golden and tender. Cut kernels from cobs.
3 Meanwhile, heat remaining oil in a large heavy-based frying pan over high heat. Cook chicken, onion, garlic, chilli and spices, stirring, for 7 minutes or until browned. Add half the tomatoes and bring to a simmer; cook for 10 minutes. Add juice and half the corn; season to taste.
4 Spoon chicken mixture onto the centre of each tortilla. Divide 1 cup cheddar evenly among tortillas; roll to enclose filling. Place in a single layer in an oiled 20cm x 30cm ovenproof dish. Spoon over remaining tomatoes, leaving ends of tortillas exposed.
5 Scatter tortillas with remaining cheddar. Bake for 15 minutes until golden. Top with remaining corn and the coriander. Serve with lime wedges.

Enchiladas can be frozen at the end of step 4 for up to 2 months; thaw in the fridge overnight, cover, then cook in a 180°C oven for 30 minutes until piping hot. Uncover for the last 10 minutes for cheese to brown.

SWAP IT!

To make this vegetarian, swap the chicken for a 400g can each drained and rinsed kidney beans and black beans, adding with the tomatoes in step 3.

THESE MEATBALLS ARE DELICIOUS ON THEIR OWN, EVEN WHEN COLD!

Chicken Meatballs

PREP + COOK TIME 50 MINUTES SERVES 4

⅔ cup (80g) frozen peas
1 teaspoon finely grated lemon rind
¼ cup chopped fresh mint leaves
350g chicken mince
2 cloves garlic, crushed
½ cup (50g) dried multigrain breadcrumbs
1 egg, beaten lightly
⅓ cup (80g) ricotta
2 tablespoons olive oil
2 x 400g cans diced tomatoes
3 teaspoons balsamic vinegar
250g spaghetti
2 tablespoons fresh mint leaves, extra
⅓ cup (25g) flaked or grated parmesan

1 Preheat oven to 240°C. Grease and line a small shallow roasting pan with baking paper.

2 Place peas in a medium heatproof bowl. Cover with boiling water and stand for 1 minute; drain, reserving 2 tablespoons of the water. Blend or process peas, reserved water, rind and chopped mint until just combined.

3 Combine chicken, garlic, breadcrumbs and egg in a medium bowl; mix well. Stir in pea mixture and ricotta.

4 Roll level tablespoons of mixture into balls using wet hands. Place in prepared pan and drizzle with oil. Roast meatballs for 15 minutes, turning once. Add tomatoes and vinegar; roast for a further 5 minutes or until the meatballs are cooked through and sauce is hot. Season sauce to taste.

5 Meanwhile, cook pasta in a large saucepan of boiling water until just tender. Drain.

6 Serve pasta with meatballs and sauce. Top with extra mint and parmesan.

You can freeze meatballs raw or cooked for up to 3 months; thaw in the fridge overnight before cooking or reheating.

FOOD FACT!
Carrots are a fantastic source of beta-carotene, which your body converts to vitamin A, essential for good eyesight.

BOMB DIGGITY BOLOGNESE

PREP + COOK TIME 25 MINUTES **SERVES** 4

- 2 tablespoons olive oil
- 2 large onions (400g), chopped
- 2 trimmed sticks celery (200g), chopped finely
- 1kg lean beef mince
- 3 cloves garlic, crushed
- 1 teaspoon dried oregano
- 4 medium carrots (500g), grated finely
- 4 medium zucchini (500g), grated coarsely
- 2 x 400g cans diced tomatoes
- 700g bottled tomato passata
- ½ cup chopped fresh basil
- 250g spaghetti

1 Heat oil in a large saucepan over medium heat. Add onion and celery; cook, stirring, for 5 minutes or until softened.

2 Increase heat to high and add beef, in two batches; cook each batch, stirring, for 5 minutes or until browned and liquid is evaporated. Add garlic, oregano, carrot and zucchini; cook, stirring, until combined and fragrant.

3 Stir in tomatoes and passata; simmer, uncovered, for 10 minutes or until thickened slightly. Add basil; season to taste with salt and pepper. Reserve half the sauce for another use (see Tip).

4 Meanwhile, add spaghetti to a large pan of boiling salted water. Boil for 8 minutes or until just tender; drain.

5 Serve spaghetti with sauce and a sprinkling of grated parmesan, if you like.

Leftover bolognese sauce can be used in tacos, nachos, quesadillas, enchiladas or burritos. Or spoon on top of roast jacket potatoes or sweet potatoes. Use as a filling in toasted sandwiches and wraps with cheese, or in the Mix 'n' Match Muffins on page 67. Freeze remaining bolognese sauce for up to 3 months; thaw in the fridge overnight before reheating.

PUMPKIN CANNELLONI

PREP + COOK TIME 1 HOUR 20 MINUTES **SERVES** 4

400g pumpkin, chopped coarsely (see Tip)
200g frozen spinach, thawed
200g ricotta cheese
12 cannelloni tubes (150g)
700g bottled tomato passata
½ cup (60g) coarsely grated cheddar cheese
½ cup (40g) finely grated parmesan cheese

1 Preheat oven to 200°C. Oil a shallow 1.5-litre (6-cup) ovenproof dish.

2 Boil, steam or microwave pumpkin until tender; drain. Mash pumpkin in a medium bowl until smooth; cool.

3 Squeeze excess liquid from spinach; chop coarsely. Stir spinach and ricotta into pumpkin; season to taste. Fill cannelloni tubes with pumpkin mixture.

4 Spread half the passata over base of dish; top with cannelloni, in a single layer. Pour remaining sauce over cannelloni; scatter with combined cheddar and parmesan.

5 Cover dish with foil; bake for 35 minutes. Uncover; bake for another 20 minutes or until cannelloni are tender and cheese is browned lightly.

SERVING SUGGESTION

Serve with a leafy green salad.

I used butternut pumpkin for this recipe. The cannelloni can be frozen for up to 2 months at the end of step 4; thaw in the fridge overnight, then continue with step 5.

FOOD FACT!
Pumpkins are a rich source of vital antioxidants. They also contain more fibre than kale and more potassium than bananas.

SALMON PATTIES

PREP + COOK TIME 40 MINUTES SERVES 4

- 2 x 200g skinless salmon fillets, halved crossways
- 1 cup (250ml) water
- ¾ cup (150g) couscous
- 1 tablespoon olive oil
- 2 green onions, sliced
- ¼ cup coarsely chopped fresh flat-leaf parsley
- 2 eggs, beaten lightly
- 45g packet lemon and herb dukkah, plus extra to serve
- ¼ cup (60ml) olive oil, extra
- ⅔ cup (190g) Greek-style yoghurt
- 1 lemon, cut into cheeks
- cucumber, asparagus and carrot, or salad, to serve

1 Place salmon and the water in a medium saucepan; bring to the boil. Remove from heat; stand for 10 minutes. Remove salmon from poaching liquid to a plate.

2 Bring poaching liquid back to the boil. Remove from heat; stir in couscous. Stand, covered, for 5 minutes or until liquid is absorbed. Fluff grains with a fork. Place couscous in a medium bowl with oil; mix well. Add flaked salmon, green onion, parsley and half the beaten egg; season. With wet hands, shape mixture into eight patties; place on a baking-paper-lined oven tray.

3 Place remaining egg and dukkah in separate small bowls. Dip patties in egg, draining off excess, then coat in dukkah.

4 Heat half the extra oil in a large frying pan over medium heat; cook half the patties for 3 minutes each side or until golden and heated through. Drain on paper towel. Repeat with remaining oil and patties.

5 Serve patties with yoghurt, lemon and vegetables or salad.

Patties can be made to the end of step 3 a day ahead. You can freeze the patties for up to 1 month; thaw in the fridge overnight, then continue from step 4.

FOOD FACT!
The salmon in this recipe delivers omega-3 essential fatty acids for brain development, at the same time adding texture and delicious flavour to the patties.

DID YOU KNOW?
Long chillies are usually mild but can vary in their heat intensity. If you scrape out the seeds and use the flesh only, you will add the flavour without the heat.

COCONUT CHICKEN CURRY

PREP + COOK TIME 50 MINUTES SERVES 6

2 fresh long green chillies, seeded, chopped
1 large onion (200g), chopped
5cm piece fresh ginger (25g), chopped
4 cloves garlic, chopped
1 tablespoon ground coriander
1 tablespoon ground cumin
1 teaspoon salt
1kg chicken thigh fillets
270ml can coconut milk
2 cups (500ml) chicken stock
600g orange sweet potato, unpeeled, cut into 2.5cm pieces
300g broccoli, chopped
100g baby spinach
⅓ cup (50g) roasted salted cashews
1 cup (280g) Greek-style yoghurt
¼ cup coarsely chopped fresh mint
1 lime, cut into wedges

1 To make curry paste, blend chilli, onion, ginger, garlic, spices and salt until smooth.

2 Trim fat from chicken; cut chicken into 4cm pieces. Heat 2 tablespoons of the coconut milk in a large saucepan over medium heat. Add curry paste; cook, stirring, for 3 minutes or until fragrant. Add chicken; cook, stirring, for 2 minutes or until combined. Add stock and remaining coconut milk; bring to the boil. Reduce heat; simmer, covered, for 10 minutes. Add sweet potato to curry; simmer, covered, for 10 minutes.

3 Add broccoli; simmer, covered, for a further 5 minutes or until just tender. Stir in spinach until just wilted.

4 Blend cashews until ground finely; stir into curry. Stir in ¾ cup of the yoghurt and the mint. Season to taste.

5 Serve curry with remaining yoghurt, topped with extra mint, if you like, and with lime wedges.

SERVING SUGGESTION

Serve with steamed basmati or brown rice.

Curry can be frozen at the end of step 2 for up to 2 months; thaw in the fridge overnight. Bring back to the boil over medium heat, then continue from step 3.

LAMB & PUMPKIN SHEPHERD'S PIE

PREP + COOK TIME 50 MINUTES SERVES 4

- 1 tablespoon olive oil
- 400g lean lamb mince
- 1 medium leek (350g), chopped finely
- 2 medium carrots (240g), chopped finely
- 4 small cloves garlic, crushed
- 2 tablespoons tomato paste
- 2 tablespoons wholemeal flour
- 2 cups (500ml) salt-reduced beef stock
- 1 tablespoon Worcestershire sauce
- 700g butternut pumpkin, peeled, chopped coarsely
- ¼ cup (60ml) milk
- 2 tablespoons pepitas (pumpkin seed kernels)
- 1 tablespoon fresh flat-leaf parsley leaves (optional)

1 Heat the oil in a large heavy-based frying pan over high heat. Add lamb; cook, stirring to break up clumps, for 5 minutes. Transfer to a large heatproof bowl, using a slotted spoon, leaving the fat in the pan.

2 Add leek and carrot to pan; cook for 2 minutes or until softened. Add garlic and tomato paste; cook, stirring, for 1 minute. Stir in flour, then return lamb to pan with stock and Worcestershire sauce; bring mixture to the boil. Reduce heat to medium; cook, stirring occasionally, for 20 minutes or until sauce thickens slightly. Divide lamb mixture among four 1½-cup (375ml) ovenproof dishes.

3 Meanwhile, preheat oven to 200°C.

4 Steam or microwave pumpkin until tender. Drain; transfer to a bowl. Add milk; mash until smooth. Season to taste. Spoon mashed pumpkin over lamb mixture; place dishes on an oven tray.

5 Bake pies for 10 minutes. Scatter with pepitas and bake for a further 5 minutes. Top with parsley to serve.

Pies can be frozen at the end of step 4 for up to 2 months; thaw in the fridge overnight, then continue with step 5, baking, covered, for 25 minutes or until pies are hot in the centre.

Party time

MINI PIZZAS WITH 3 TOPPINGS

PREP + COOK TIME 40 MINUTES MAKES 12

12 small wholemeal pita or wraps (300g)

VEGGIE

50g button mushrooms
¼ cup (30g) pitted black olives (optional)
½ cup (120g) chargrilled capsicum
⅓ cup (50g) semi-dried tomatoes
1½ cups (150g) pizza cheese

TANDOORI CHICKEN

1½ cups (150g) pizza cheese
2 cups (320g) shredded cooked chicken
¼ cup (60ml) tandoori paste
¼ cup (70g) Greek-style yoghurt
1 cup (85g) small broccoli florets

BURGER

1½ cups (150g) pizza cheese
300g beef mince
2 pickled dill cucumbers, sliced (optional)

Each of the toppings makes enough for 4 mini pizza bases.

1 Preheat oven to 200°C. Line two oven trays with baking paper.

2 Place bases on oven trays. Top with your choice of topping below. Bake for 20 minutes or until cheese melts and bases are crisp.

VEGGIE

Thinly slice mushrooms, olives, capsicum and tomatoes. Scatter 1 cup of the cheese over 4 bases. Top with mushrooms, olives, capsicum and tomato, then remaining cheese.

TANDOORI CHICKEN

Scatter 1 cup of the cheese over 4 bases. Toss chicken with combined paste and yoghurt. Top bases with chicken and remaining cheese. Add broccoli in the last 10 minutes of cooking time.

BURGER

Scatter 1 cup of the cheese over bases. Roll mince into small balls and flatten slightly. Top bases with balls and season. Scatter with remaining cheese. Serve topped with pickled dill cucumbers.

2
1

TIGER WEDGES

PREP + COOK TIME 50 MINUTES **SERVES** 8

500g potatoes, unpeeled, washed
500g small orange sweet potatoes, unpeeled, washed
2 tablespoons garlic and herb seasoning (see Swap It)
2 tablespoons olive oil

1 Preheat oven to 240°C. Oil an oven tray.
2 Cut potatoes and sweet potatoes into wedges lengthways. Place in a large bowl with seasoning and oil; toss to coat (see Tip).
3 Place wedges, in a single layer, on oven tray. Roast for 40 minutes or until wedges are tender and browned.

SERVING SUGGESTIONS

Serve wedges with aioli or mayonnaise, or a low-sugar tomato sauce, or you can make the tomato dipping sauce on page 167.

You can shake the wedges, seasoning and oil together in a clean resealable plastic bag; ensure each wedge is seasoned all over.

SWAP IT!

For a variation, swap the garlic and herb seasoning for sea salt and sweet paprika; add these to the bowl with the potatoes and oil in step 2.

MINI MEATBALLS

PREP + COOK TIME 45 MINUTES MAKES 50

1kg beef mince
1 cup (70g) stale breadcrumbs
½ cup (40g) grated parmesan cheese
2 cloves garlic, crushed
2 green onions, chopped
1 tablespoon Worcestershire sauce
2 tablespoons tomato dipping sauce (see below)
2 tablespoons olive oil

TOMATO DIPPING SAUCE

1 tablespoon olive oil
1 medium onion (150g), chopped
2 cloves garlic, crushed
400g can diced tomatoes
1 teaspoon unrefined sugar

1 Make tomato dipping sauce.

2 Combine mince, breadcrumbs, cheese, garlic, onion and sauces in a large bowl; shape level tablespoons of mixture into balls. You can make the balls larger, if you like.

3 Heat oil in a large frying pan over medium-high heat; cook meatballs, in batches, for 6 minutes or until browned and cooked through, shaking the pan occasionally.

4 Serve meatballs with tomato dipping sauce.

tomato dipping sauce Heat oil in a small saucepan over medium heat. Cook onion, stirring occasionally, for 5 minutes or until softened. Add garlic; cook for 1 minute. Add undrained tomatoes and sugar; simmer, uncovered, for 10 minutes or until thickened. Blend sauce briefly until just smooth. Season to taste. Return to pan and reheat sauce just before serving.

Meatballs can be cooked a day ahead. Reheat on oven trays, covered loosely with foil, in a 180°C oven for 10 minutes. Uncooked meatballs can be frozen for up to 3 months.

THESE NUGGETS ARE A HEALTHY TAKE ON THE TRADITIONAL PARTY FARE.

CHICKEN NUGGETS

PREP + COOK TIME 30 MINUTES **MAKES** 20

- 2 eggs
- 2 cups (190g) quinoa flakes
- ½ cup (60g) almond meal or fine breadcrumbs
- 500g chicken breast fillets, chopped into nugget-sized pieces
- olive oil cooking spray
- low-sugar tomato sauce, to serve

1 Preheat oven to 180°C. Line an oven tray with baking paper.

2 Beat eggs lightly in a shallow bowl. Place combined quinoa flakes and almond meal in a separate shallow bowl; season.

3 Dip chicken, one piece at a time, into the egg and then press into the quinoa mixture to firmly coat. Place on tray. Spray with olive oil.

4 Bake nuggets for 20 minutes or until browned and cooked through.

5 Serve chicken nuggets with tomato sauce.

FOOD FACT!
Quinoa is rich in many essential minerals, such as calcium, iron, phosphorous, potassium, magnesium, sodium and zinc.

CHOC BEET CAKE

PREP + COOK TIME 1 HOUR 25 MINUTES (+ STANDING) **SERVES** 10

120g dark chocolate (70% cocoa), chopped
1½ cups (240g) coconut sugar
½ cup (125ml) coconut oil
4 eggs, at room temperature, beaten lightly
½ cup (60g) desiccated coconut
2 cups (300g) coarsely grated fresh beetroot (see Tip)
1 teaspoon vanilla extract
1¼ cups (160g) quinoa flour
2 tablespoons cacao powder
2 teaspoons baking powder
2 teaspoons ground cinnamon
250g firm ricotta
¼ cup (60ml) pure maple syrup
¼ cup grated fresh beetroot, extra (optional) (see Tip)
50g block dark chocolate (70% cocoa), extra (optional)

1 Preheat oven to 170°C. Grease a deep 20cm round cake pan; line base with baking paper.

2 Place chocolate, sugar and oil in a medium heatproof bowl over a saucepan of simmering water; don't let the base of the bowl touch the water. Stir for 3 minutes or until chocolate is melted and mixture is smooth. Cool for 5 minutes. Stir in eggs, coconut, beetroot and vanilla.

3 Sift flour, cacao, baking powder and cinnamon into a medium bowl; gently fold into chocolate mixture. Spoon into pan; level surface. Bake for 50 minutes or until a skewer inserted into the centre comes out clean. Leave in pan for 15 minutes; turn out onto a wire rack to cool.

4 To make frosting, process ricotta and maple syrup until smooth. Squeeze 1 tablespoon of juice from extra beetroot with your hand; swirl beetroot juice through frosting and spread over cake. Run a vegetable peeler down the side of the extra block of chocolate to make curls; scatter on top of cake, if you like.

You will need 2 large beetroot (400g) for the whole recipe. Un-iced cake can be made up to 3 days ahead; store in an airtight container. Refrigerate once frosted.

FOOD FACT!

Beets are high in immune-boosting vitamin C and potassium, the latter of which is essential for healthy nerve and muscle function.

FOOD FACT!

Blueberries contain more vitamin C than oranges, and raspberries have one of the highest concentrations of antioxidants of any fruit on earth.

CHOC-BERRY BROWNIES

COOK + PREP TIME 45 MINUTES MAKES 24

1 cup (120g) almond meal
½ cup (50g) chocolate protein powder
¾ cup (75g) cacao powder
¼ teaspoon Himalayan salt
½ cup (100g) coconut oil
1 cup (250ml) rice malt syrup
1 cup (280g) unsweetened apple sauce or puree
1 teaspoon vanilla extract
2 eggs
2 egg whites
125g blueberries or berries of your choice
extra berries, to serve (optional)

1 Preheat oven to 180°C. Grease a 20cm x 30cm slice pan; line the base with baking paper.
2 Combine almond meal, sifted protein powder, cacao and salt in a medium bowl.
3 Heat oil and syrup in a medium saucepan over medium heat until melted. Remove from heat; stand for 5 minutes to cool slightly.
4 Whisk sauce and vanilla into syrup mixture, then eggs and egg whites, one at a time, whisking after each addition. Add egg mixture to flour mixture; whisk until combined. Fold in berries. Pour into pan.
5 Bake for 30 minutes or until a skewer inserted into the centre comes out clean. Cool in pan.
6 Cut into 24 pieces. Serve scattered with extra berries.

CINNAMON DONUT POPCORN

PREP + COOK TIME 5 MINUTES MAKES 8 CUPS

- ¼ cup (60ml) mild-flavoured extra virgin olive oil
- ½ cup (120g) popping corn
- 1½ tablespoons Natvia (see Tip)
- 3 teaspoons ground cinnamon
- ½ teaspoon sea salt flakes, crushed lightly

1 Heat 1 tablespoon of the oil in a large saucepan over medium heat. Add the popping corn; cover pan with lid. Cook, shaking the pan occasionally, for 4 minutes or until the popping stops. Transfer the popcorn to a large bowl, leaving behind any unpopped corn in the pan.

2 Meanwhile, combine remaining oil, Natvia, cinnamon and salt in a small bowl.

3 Drizzle popcorn with spice mixture; toss well to coat.

Natvia is a 100% natural sweetener made with organic stevia; it has minimal effect on blood glucose levels. Popcorn can be made up to 3 days ahead; store in an airtight container.

TICKET
ADMIT ONE PERSON
00244
ADMIT ONE PERSON
00246
TICKET
ADMIT ONE PERSON
00245
TICKET

Gingerbread Twins

PREP + COOK TIME **50 MINUTES (+ FREEZING & COOLING)** **MAKES** **10 TWINS**

- 1½ cups (240g) wholemeal plain flour
- 1 cup (150g) white plain flour
- 1 tablespoon ground ginger
- 1 teaspoon bicarbonate of soda
- 8 fresh pitted dates (160g), halved
- 1 egg
- ⅓ cup (70g) coconut oil, melted
- ½ cup (125ml) rice malt syrup or brown rice syrup
- 1 teaspoon vanilla extract
- 50g dark chocolate (70% cocoa), melted (optional)

1 Process dry ingredients and dates until dates are finely chopped. Add egg, oil, syrup and vanilla; process until mixture comes together and forms a soft dough.

2 Divide dough in half. Roll each half between sheets of baking paper until 20cm x 30cm in size and 3mm thick. Slide dough, on baking paper, onto trays; freeze for 20 minutes or until firm enough to hold its shape.

3 Preheat the oven to 180°C. Line two large oven trays with baking paper.

4 Cut out as many gingerbread men shapes as possible, using an 8cm x 9cm cutter. Transfer shapes to trays. Gather up scraps and knead lightly. Re-roll and repeat from step 2. Cut remaining scraps of dough into small heart shapes. Join some of the shapes with a heart and join some hands.

5 Bake gingerbread twins for 12 minutes or until browned, turning trays halfway through cooking time. Cool on trays.

6 Place chocolate in a small piping bag fitted with a small tube. Decorate shapes with chocolate as desired, or let the children decorate their own. Stand until set.

Gingerbread twins will keep in an airtight container for up to 1 week.

FOOD FACT!
Raspberries are considered a superfood and have multiple health benefits, including boosting cardiovascular and liver functions.

RASPBERRY RIPPLE YOGHURT POPS

PREP + COOK TIME 15 MINUTES (+ FREEZING) **MAKES** 6

- 150g fresh or frozen raspberries
- 1 tablespoon lemon juice (see Tip)
- 2 tablespoons honey
- 1 vanilla bean
- 1 cup (280g) Greek-style yoghurt
- 1 teaspoon finely grated lemon rind (see Tip)
- 1½ tablespoons honey, extra

1 Place raspberries, juice and honey in a medium bowl; crush berries using a fork. Spoon 1 tablespoon of the raspberry mixture into each base of six ⅓-cup (80ml) dariole moulds, paper cups or popsicle containers. Freeze for 1 hour or until firm.

2 Meanwhile, split vanilla bean in half lengthways; scrape seeds into a medium bowl. Whisk in yoghurt, rind and extra honey until combined. Fold in remaining raspberry mixture to form a ripple effect.

3 Divide mixture among moulds. Insert a popsicle stick into each one. Freeze overnight.

4 To serve, dip moulds quickly in hot water and turn out.

It's easier to finely grate the rind from the lemon before you squeeze the juice. Pops can be made up to a week ahead.

Little Carrot Party Cupcakes

PREP + COOK TIME 55 MINUTES (+ COOLING) **MAKES** 12

⅓ cup (35g) sultanas
¼ cup (60ml) boiling water
2 eggs
¾ cup (185g) Natvia
¼ cup (85g) rice malt syrup
⅔ cup (140g) virgin coconut oil, melted
2 teaspoons vanilla extract
2 cups (340g) firmly packed coarsely grated carrot (see Tip)
½ cup (60g) chopped pecans, roasted (optional)
1⅔ cups (250g) self-raising flour
½ teaspoon bicarbonate of soda
3 teaspoons ground cinnamon
1 teaspoon ground ginger
assorted fruit, to decorate

DATE CREAM CHEESE FROSTING

125g dried pitted dates, chopped finely
2 tablespoons boiling water
250g cream cheese, softened
125g ricotta

You need about 2½ medium carrots to make 2 cups of grated carrot.

1 Preheat oven to 180°C. Line a 12-hole (⅓-cup/80ml) muffin pan with paper cases.

2 Place sultanas in a small heatproof bowl; pour over the boiling water and stand for 10 minutes.

3 Meanwhile, whisk eggs, Natvia, syrup, oil and vanilla in a small bowl with an electric mixer for 5 minutes. Transfer mixture to a large bowl; stir in carrot, sultanas and soaking liquid, then pecans and sifted dry ingredients. Divide mixture evenly among paper cases.

4 Bake cakes for 20 minutes or until a skewer inserted into the centre of one comes out clean. Turn cakes, top-side up, onto a wire rack to cool.

5 Meanwhile, make date cream cheese frosting. Place frosting in a piping bag fitted with a 1cm tube; pipe on top of cooled cakes. Decorate cupcakes with assorted fruit.

date cream cheese frosting Process dates and the boiling water until almost smooth, scraping down the side of the bowl. Add cream cheese and ricotta; process, scraping down the side of the bowl, until frosting is combined.

GLOSSARY

ACAI (pronounced ah-sigh-ee) a small, round fruit with a large, hard, inedible pit and a dark-purple, pulpy skin, that tastes like a blend of berries and chocolate. Jam-packed full of antioxidants.

ALMONDS

flaked paper-thin slices of blanched or natural almonds.

meal powdered to a coarse flour-like texture.

BAKING POWDER a raising agent consisting mainly of two parts cream of tartar to one part bicarbonate of soda.

BEANS

black also called turtle beans or black kidney beans; an earthy-flavoured dried bean completely different from the better-known Chinese black beans (fermented soybeans). Used mostly in Mexican and South American cooking.

kidney medium-size red bean, slightly floury in texture yet sweet in flavour; sold dried or canned. Found in bean mixes and is used in chilli con carne.

BICARBONATE OF SODA a raising agent.

BREADCRUMBS

packaged prepared fine-textured but crunchy white breadcrumbs; good for coating foods that are to be fried.

panko (Japanese) are available in two kinds: larger pieces and fine crumbs; they are lighter in texture than Western-style breadcrumbs. Available from Asian food stores and most supermarkets.

stale crumbs made by grating, blending or processing 1- or 2-day-old bread.

CACAO POWDER raw cacao powder is made by removing the cocoa butter, using a process known as cold-pressing. It retains more of its nutrients than heat-processed cocoa powder; it also has a stronger, more bitter chocolate taste.

CHEESE

cheddar the most common cow's milk 'tasty' cheese; should be aged, hard and have a pronounced bite.

cream commonly called Philadelphia or Philly; a soft cow's milk cheese, its fat content ranges from 14% to 33%.

feta Greek in origin; a crumbly textured goat's or sheep's milk cheese with a sharp, salty taste. Ripened and stored in salted whey.

haloumi a Greek Cypriot cheese with a semi-firm, spongy texture and very salty-sweet flavour. Ripened and stored in salted whey; best grilled or fried, it holds its shape well on being heated. Eat while still warm, as it becomes tough and rubbery on cooling.

parmesan also called parmigiano; is a hard, grainy cow's milk cheese originating in Italy. Reggiano is the best variety.

pizza a blend of grated mozzarella, cheddar and parmesan cheeses.

ricotta a soft, sweet, moist, white cow's milk cheese with a low fat content and a slightly grainy texture. The name roughly translates as 'cooked again' and refers to ricotta's manufacture from a whey that is itself a by-product of other cheese-making.

CHIA SEEDS contain protein and all the essential amino acids, and a wealth of vitamins, minerals and antioxidants, as well as being fibre-rich.

CHICKPEAS irregularly round, sandy-coloured type of legume.

CHOCOLATE, DARK also called semi-sweet or luxury chocolate; made of a high percentage of cocoa liquor and cocoa butter, and little added sugar. Unless stated otherwise, I use dark eating chocolate as it's ideal for use in desserts and cakes.

CINNAMON available both in the piece (called sticks or quills) and ground into powder; one of the world's most common spices, used universally as a sweet, fragrant flavouring for both sweet and savoury foods.

COCONUT

cream obtained commercially from the first pressing of the coconut flesh alone, without the addition of water; the second pressing (less rich) is sold as coconut milk. Available in cans and cartons at most supermarkets.

desiccated concentrated, dried, unsweetened and finely shredded coconut flesh.

flaked dried flaked coconut flesh.

milk not the liquid found inside the fruit (coconut water), but the diluted liquid from the second pressing of the white flesh of a mature coconut (the first pressing produces coconut cream). Available in cans and cartons at most supermarkets.

oil is extracted from the coconut flesh so you don't get any of the fibre, protein or carbohydrates present in the whole coconut. The best quality is virgin coconut oil, which is the oil pressed from the dried coconut flesh, and doesn't include the use of solvents or other refining processes.

shredded unsweetened thin strips of dried coconut flesh.

sugar is not made from coconuts but the sap of the blossoms of the coconut palm tree. The refined sap looks a little like raw or light brown sugar and has a similar caramel flavour. It also has the same amount of kilojoules as regular white sugar.

CORIANDER also known as pak chee or Chinese parsley; a bright-green leafy herb with a pungent flavour. Both stems and roots of coriander are also used in cooking; wash well before using. Also available ground or as seeds; these should not be substituted for fresh as the tastes are completely different.

CORNFLOUR available made from corn (maize so gluten-free) or from wheat (contains gluten). Can either be used in baking, or as a thickening agent in cooking.

COUSCOUS a fine, grain-like cereal product made from semolina. A semolina flour and water dough is sieved then dehydrated to produce minuscule even-sized pellets of couscous; it is rehydrated by steaming or with the addition of a warm liquid and swells 3–4 times in size.

CUMIN also known as zeera or comino; resembling caraway in size, cumin is the dried seed of a plant related to the parsley family. Its spicy, almost curry-like flavour is essential to the traditional foods of Mexico, India, North Africa and the Middle East. Available dried as seeds or ground. Black cumin seeds are smaller than standard cumin, and dark brown rather than true black.

CURRY POWDER a blend of ground spices used for making Indian and some South-East Asian dishes. Consists of dried chilli, cumin, cinnamon, coriander, fennel, mace, fenugreek, cardamom and turmeric. Available mild or hot.

DIJON MUSTARD pale brown, distinctively flavoured, fairly mild-tasting French mustard.

DUKKAH an Egyptian specialty spice mixture made up of roasted nuts, seeds and an array of aromatic spices.

FISH SAUCE naam pla (Thai) and nuoc naam (Vietnamese) are almost identical varieties. Made from pulverised salted fermented fish (most often anchovies); has a pungent smell and strong taste. There are many versions of varying intensity, so use according to your taste.

GINGER

fresh also called green or root ginger; the thick gnarled root of a tropical plant. Can be kept peeled, covered with dry sherry in a jar and refrigerated, or frozen in an airtight container.

ground also called powdered ginger; used as a flavouring in baking but cannot be substituted for fresh ginger.

LEMONGRASS a tall, clumping, lemon-smelling and -tasting, sharp-edged grass; only the white part of the stem is used.

LSA a ground mixture of linseeds (L), sunflower seeds (S) and almonds (A); available from supermarkets and health food stores.

MAPLE SYRUP, PURE distilled from the sap of sugar maple trees found only in Canada and the USA. Maple-flavoured or pancake syrup is not an adequate substitute.

OIL

coconut see *coconut*

oil spray I use olive oil spray.

olive made from ripened olives. Extra virgin and virgin are the first and second press of the olives; 'light' refers to taste not fat levels.

sesame used as a flavouring rather than a cooking medium.

ORANGE SWEET POTATO an orange-fleshed sweet potato often confused with yam.

PAPRIKA ground, dried, sweet red capsicum; there are many grades and types available, including sweet, hot, mild and smoked.

PEPITAS (PUMPKIN SEED KERNELS) the green kernels (seeds) of dried pumpkin seeds; available plain or salted.

POLENTA also known as cornmeal; a flour-like cereal made of ground corn (maize). Also the name of the dish made from it.

QUINOA (pronouced keen-wa) A seed not a grain with a delicate, slightly nutty taste and chewy texture. Quinoa is gluten-free.

RICE MALT SYRUP also known as brown rice syrup or rice syrup; is made by cooking brown rice flour with enzymes to break down its starch into sugars from which the water is removed.

ROCKET also known as arugula, rugula and rucola; a peppery green leaf eaten raw in salads or used in cooking. Baby rocket leaves are smaller and less peppery.

SESAME SEEDS black and white are the most common of this small oval seed; however, there are also red and brown varieties. The seeds are used in cuisines around the world as an ingredient and as a condiment.

SOY SAUCE also known as sieu; made from fermented soybeans. Several variations are available in supermarkets and Asian grocery stores; I use Japanese soy sauce unless indicated otherwise.

SPINACH also, incorrectly, called silverbeet. Its thick, soft oval leaves and stems are both edible.

STEVIA comes from the leaves of a plant so is promoted as a natural sweetener. It is processed into a white powder that can be used in a similar way to sugar. It has a minimal effect on blood glucose levels so can be a useful way to reduce your sugar intake.

SUNFLOWER SEEDS grey-green, slightly soft, oily kernels; a nutritious snack.

TAHINI a rich, sesame-seed paste; available from supermarkets and health food stores.

TAMARI a thick, dark soy sauce made mainly from soybeans but without the wheat used in most standard soy sauces.

VANILLA EXTRACT obtained from vanilla beans infused in water; a non-alcoholic version of essence.

WOMBOK (NAPA CABBAGE) also known as Chinese cabbage or Peking cabbage; elongated in shape with pale green, crinkly leaves, this is the most common cabbage in South-East Asia. Can be shredded or chopped and eaten raw or braised, steamed or stir-fried.

WORCESTERSHIRE SAUCE this dark-coloured condiment is made from garlic, lime, soy sauce, tamarind, onions, molasses, anchovies, vinegar and seasonings.

YOGHURT, GREEK-STYLE plain yoghurt that has been strained in a cloth (muslin) to remove the whey and to give it a creamy consistency.

CONVERSION CHART

MEASURES

One Australian metric measuring cup holds approximately 250ml; one Australian metric tablespoon holds 20ml; one Australian metric teaspoon holds 5ml. The difference between one country's measuring cups and another's is within a two- or three-teaspoon variance and will not affect your cooking results. North America, New Zealand and the United Kingdom use a 15ml tablespoon. All cup and spoon measurements are level. The most accurate way of measuring dry ingredients is to weigh them. When measuring liquids, use a clear glass or plastic jug with the metric markings. I use large eggs with an average weight of 60g.

DRY MEASURES

METRIC	IMPERIAL
15g	½ oz
30g	1oz
60g	2oz
90g	3oz
125g	4oz (¼ lb)
155g	5oz
185g	6oz
220g	7oz
250g	8oz (½ lb)
280g	9oz
315g	10oz
345g	11oz
375g	12oz (¾ lb)
410g	13oz
440g	14oz
470g	15oz
500g	16oz (1lb)
750g	24oz (1½ lb)
1kg	32oz (2lb)

LIQUID MEASURES

METRIC	IMPERIAL
30ml	1 fluid oz
60ml	2 fluid oz
100ml	3 fluid oz
125ml	4 fluid oz
150ml	5 fluid oz
190ml	6 fluid oz
250ml	8 fluid oz
300ml	10 fluid oz
500ml	16 fluid oz
600ml	20 fluid oz
1000ml (1 litre)	1¾ pints

LENGTH MEASURES

METRIC	IMPERIAL
3mm	⅛ in
6mm	¼ in
1cm	½ in
2cm	¾ in
2.5cm	1in
5cm	2in
6cm	2½ in
8cm	3in
10cm	4in
13cm	5in
15cm	6in
18cm	7in
20cm	8in
22cm	9in
25cm	10in
28cm	11in
30cm	12in (1ft)

OVEN TEMPERATURES

The oven temperatures in this book are for conventional ovens; if you have a fan-forced oven, decrease the temperature by 10–20 degrees.

	°C (Celsius)	°F (Fahrenheit)
Very slow	120	250
Slow	150	300
Moderately slow	160	325
Moderate	180	350
Moderately hot	200	400
Hot	220	425
Very hot	240	475

INDEX

A

B

C

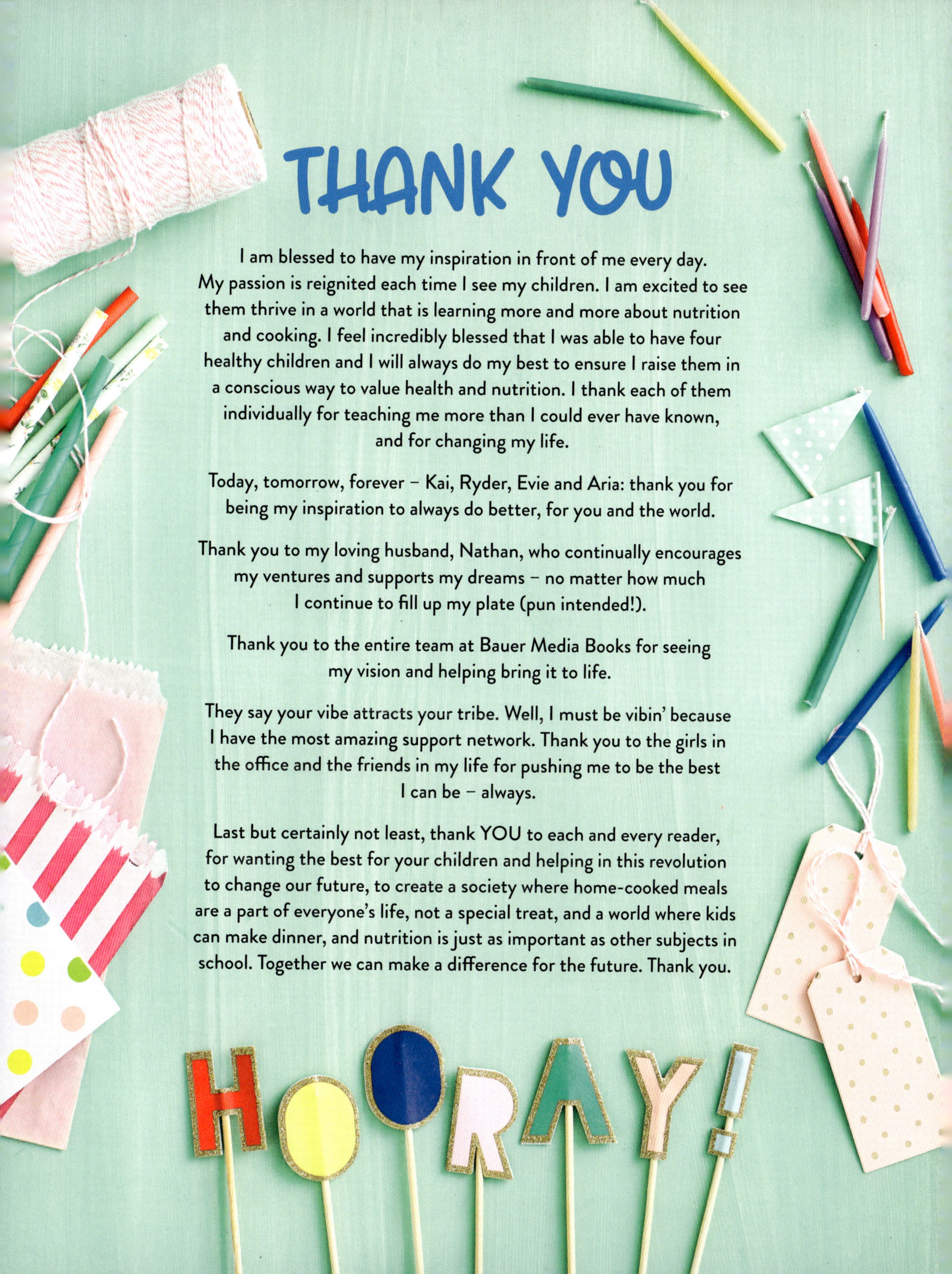

THANK YOU

I am blessed to have my inspiration in front of me every day. My passion is reignited each time I see my children. I am excited to see them thrive in a world that is learning more and more about nutrition and cooking. I feel incredibly blessed that I was able to have four healthy children and I will always do my best to ensure I raise them in a conscious way to value health and nutrition. I thank each of them individually for teaching me more than I could ever have known, and for changing my life.

Today, tomorrow, forever – Kai, Ryder, Evie and Aria: thank you for being my inspiration to always do better, for you and the world.

Thank you to my loving husband, Nathan, who continually encourages my ventures and supports my dreams – no matter how much I continue to fill up my plate (pun intended!).

Thank you to the entire team at Bauer Media Books for seeing my vision and helping bring it to life.

They say your vibe attracts your tribe. Well, I must be vibin' because I have the most amazing support network. Thank you to the girls in the office and the friends in my life for pushing me to be the best I can be – always.

Last but certainly not least, thank YOU to each and every reader, for wanting the best for your children and helping in this revolution to change our future, to create a society where home-cooked meals are a part of everyone's life, not a special treat, and a world where kids can make dinner, and nutrition is just as important as other subjects in school. Together we can make a difference for the future. Thank you.

PUBLISHED IN 2018 BY BAUER MEDIA BOOKS, AUSTRALIA.
BAUER MEDIA BOOKS IS A DIVISION OF BAUER MEDIA PTY LTD.

Bauer Media Books

PUBLISHER SALLY EAGLE

EDITORIAL & FOOD DIRECTOR
SOPHIA YOUNG

CREATIVE DIRECTOR
HANNAH BLACKMORE

MANAGING EDITOR
STEPHANIE KISTNER

SENIOR DESIGNER
ALEXANDRA COOK

SENIOR EDITOR CHANTAL GIBBS

FOOD EDITOR ALEXANDRA ELLIOTT

RECIPE DEVELOPER NADIA FONOFF

OPERATIONS MANAGER
DAVID SCOTTO

FOOD PHOTOGRAPHY

PHOTOGRAPHER JOHN PAUL URIZAR

STYLISTS JENN TOLHURST,
KATE BROWN

PHOTOCHEFS TESSA IMMENS,
REBECCA CLANCY,
SARAH-JANE HALLET

COVER & LOCATION PHOTOGRAPHY

LOCATION TEMPLE FARMHOUSE,
BYRON BAY, NSW

PHOTOGRAPHY WISE PHOTOGRAPHY

STYLIST SARAH DE NARDI

PHOTOCHEF AMAL WEBSTER

HAIR MINOGUE HAIRDRESSING

AUTHOR SOPHIE GUIDOLIN
WWW.SOPHIEGUIDOLIN.COM.AU

I WOULD LIKE TO THANK THE FOLLOWING BRANDS FOR THEIR HELP WITH THE PHOTOSHOOT:

BEAU HUDSON FOR WARDROBE
WWW.BEAUHUDSON.CO

ROCK YOUR BABY FOR WARDROBE
ROCKYOURBABY.COM

GRITCERAMICS FOR PROPS
WWW.GRITCERAMICS.COM

Printed in China by Leo Paper Products Ltd

Published by Bauer Media Books
a division of Bauer Media Pty Ltd,
54 Park St, Sydney; GPO Box 4088,
Sydney, NSW 2001, Australia
ph +61 2 9282 8618
fax +61 2 9126 3702
www.awwcookbooks.com.au

A catalogue record for this book is available from the National Library of Australia.

ISBN: 978-1-92569-486-4 (paperback)

To order books
www.sophieguidolin.com.au